HAVERING ~~~~~
COLLEGE LIBRARY

WITHDRAWN FROM HAVERING COLLEGES
SIXTH FORM LIBRARY

Self-Harming and Suicide

ISSUES

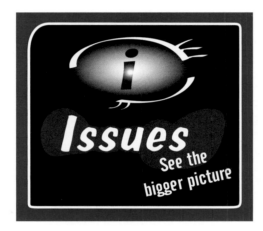

Volume 199

Series Editor

Lisa Firth

Independence

Educational Publishers

Cambridge

First published by Independence

The Studio, High Green

Great Shelford

Cambridge CB22 5EG

England

© Independence 2010

Copyright

This book is sold subject to the condition that it shall not,
by way of trade or otherwise, be lent, resold, hired out or otherwise
circulated in any form of binding or cover other than that in which it
is published without the publisher's prior consent.

Photocopy licence

The material in this book is protected by copyright. However, the
purchaser is free to make multiple copies of particular articles for instructional
purposes for immediate use within the purchasing institution.
Making copies of the entire book is not permitted.

British Library Cataloguing in Publication Data

Self-harming and suicide. -- (Issues ; v. 199)

1. Suicide--Great Britain. 2. Parasuicide--Great Britain.

3. Teenagers--Suicidal behavior--Great Britain. 4. Young

adults--Suicidal behavior--Great Britain.

I. Series II. Firth, Lisa.

362.2'8'0835'0941-dc22

ISBN-13: 978 1 86168 556 8

Printed in Great Britain

MWL Print Group Ltd

CONTENTS

Chapter 1 Self-Harm

Chapter 2 Suicide

OTHER TITLES IN THE ISSUES SERIES

For more on these titles, visit: www.independence.co.uk

EXPLORING THE ISSUES

Photocopiable study guides to accompany the above publications. Each four-page A4 guide provides a variety of discussion points and other activities to suit a wide range of ability levels and interests.

A note on critical evaluation

Because the information reprinted here is from a number of different sources, readers should bear in mind the origin of the text and whether the source is likely to have a particular bias when presenting information (just as they would if undertaking their own research). It is hoped that, as you read about the many aspects of the issues explored in this book, you will critically evaluate the information presented. It is important that you decide whether you are being presented with facts or opinions. Does the writer give a biased or an unbiased report? If an opinion is being expressed, do you agree with the writer?

Self-Harming and Suicide offers a useful starting point for those who need convenient access to information about the many issues involved. However, it is only a starting point. Following each article is a URL to the relevant organisation's website, which you may wish to visit for further information.

Self-harm

**Information from the Royal College of Psychiatrists.**

This article provides information about self-harm and is for anyone who is harming themselves, or feels that they might. We hope it will also be helpful for their friends and families.

What is self-harm?

Self-harm happens when someone hurts or harms themselves. They may:

⇨ take too many tablets;

⇨ cut themselves;

⇨ burn their body;

⇨ bang their head;

⇨ throw their body against something hard;

⇨ punch themselves;

⇨ stick things in their body;

⇨ swallow inappropriate objects.

It can feel to other people that these things are done coolly and deliberately – almost cynically. But someone who self-harms will usually do it in a state of high emotion, distress and unbearable inner turmoil. Some people plan it in advance, others do it suddenly. Some people self-harm only once or twice, but others do it regularly – it can become almost like an addiction.

Some of us harm ourselves in less obvious – but still serious – ways. We may behave in ways that suggest we don't care whether we live or die – we may take drugs recklessly, have unsafe sex, or binge drink. Some people simply starve themselves.

Other words that are used to describe self-harm

These terms are inaccurate and going out of use:

⇨ Deliberate self-harm (DSH) – the word 'deliberate' unhelpfully blamed self-harm as a reaction to painful feelings.

⇨ Suicide/Parasuicide – most people who self-harm do not want to kill themselves, so these terms are misleading.

Who self-harms?

⇨ About one n ten young people will self-harm at some point, but it can occur at any age.

⇨ It is more common in young women than men.

⇨ Gay and b sexual people seem to be more likely to self-harm.

⇨ Sometimes groups of young people self-harm together – having a friend who self-harms may increase your chances of doing it as well.

- Self-harm is more common in some sub-cultures – 'goths' seem to be particularly vulnerable.
- People who self-harm are more likely to have experienced physical, emotional or sexual abuse during childhood.

Research probably under estimates how common self-harm is, and surveys find higher rates in communities and schools than in hospitals. Some types of self-harm, like cutting, may be more secret and so less likely to be noticed by other people. In a recent study of over 4,000 self-harming adults in hospital, 80% had overdosed and around 15% had cut themselves. In the community, these statistics would probably be reversed.

What makes people self-harm?

Emotional distress – people often struggle with difficulties for some time before they self-harm:

- physical or sexual abuse.
- feeling depressed.
- feeling bad about yourself.
- relationship problems with partners, friends and family.

If you feel:

- that people don't listen to you.
- hopeless.
- isolated, alone.
- out of control.
- powerless – it feels as though there's nothing you can do to change anything.

Using alcohol or drugs – it may feel that these are as out of control as the rest of your life.

If you want to show someone else how distressed you are or to get back at them or to punish them. This is not common – most people suffer in silence and self-harm in private.

How does it make you feel?

Self-harm can help you to feel in control, and reduce uncomfortable feelings of tension and distress. If you feel guilty, it can be a way of punishing yourself and relieving your guilt. Either way, it can become a 'quick fix' for feeling bad.

Are people who self-harm mentally ill?

Most people who self-harm are not mentally ill. However, some may be depressed, or have severe personality difficulties, or be addicted to alcohol and drugs. But they all still need help – the risk of killing yourself increases after self-harm. Everyone who self-harms should be taken seriously and offered help.

Getting help

A lot of people who self-harm don't ask for help. Many young people who self-harm know that they have serious problems, but don't feel that they can tell anyone – so they don't talk to friends, family, or professionals. Other young people don't feel that they have serious problems – they use self-harm as a way of coping, but their situation stays the same.

What's more, less than half of those who go to hospital after self-harming are seen by a specialist in this area. You are less likely to be seen by a specialist if you are young, if you cut yourself, or if you have taken an overdose.

Danger signs

Those who are most likely to harm themselves badly:

- use a dangerous or violent method.
- self-harm regularly.
- are socially isolated.
- have a psychiatric disorder.

They should be assessed by someone with experience of self-harm and mental health problems.

What help is there?

Talking with a non-professional

Many people find that it's helpful just to talk anonymously to someone else about what is happening to them. Knowing that someone else knows what you are going through can help you to feel less alone with your problems. It can also help you to think about your difficulties more clearly – maybe even see ways of solving them that you wouldn't think of on your own. You can do this on the Internet or by telephone.

Self-help groups

A group of people who all self-harm meet regularly to give each other emotional support and practical advice. Just sharing your problems in a group can help you to feel less alone – others in the group will almost certainly have had similar experiences.

Help with relationships

Self-harm is often the result of a crisis in a close relationship. If this is the case, help with the relationship will be needed rather than help with self-harm.

ROYAL COLLEGE OF PSYCHIATRISTS

Talking with a professional

For people who use self-harm to cope with other problems, one-to-one treatments can help. These include:

⇨ Problem-solving therapy.

⇨ Cognitive psychotherapy.

⇨ Psychodynamic psychotherapy.

⇨ Cognitive behavioural therapy.

Family meetings

Where this is appropriate, family meetings with a therapist can help to relieve the tiring, daily stress for everyone in the family.

Group therapy

This is different from a self-help group. A professional will lead (or facilitate) the group in a way that helps the members to deal with problems in getting on with other people.

What works best?

There is little evidence to say that any one of these therapies is better than any of the others for self-harm, although what evidence there is supports problem-solving therapy.

What if I don't get help?

⇨ About one in three people who self-harm for the first time will do it again during the following year.

⇨ About three in 100 people who self-harm over 15 years will actually kill themselves. This is more than 50 times the rate for people who don't self-harm. The risk increases with age and is much greater for men.

⇨ Cutting can give you permanent scarring, numbness, or weakness/paralysis of fingers.

> *About three in 100 people who self-harm over 15 years will actually kill themselves. This is more than 50 times the rate for people who don't self-harm*

⇨ The above information is an extract from the Royal College of Psychiatrists' factsheet *Self-Harm* and is reprinted with their permission. Visit www.rcpsych.ac.uk for more information or to view the full text.

© *Royal College of Psychiatrists*

Self-injury: myths and common sense

Sounds familiar? Current treatment of people who self-injure is based on inaccurate stereotypes	The responses below are based on the real experiences of self-injurers
'It's attention-seeking'	If attention was the motivation of self-injury, it's not an efficient way of getting it. There are many easier, less painful and less degrading ways of attracting it.
'It's a Borderline Personality Disorder'	Self-injury is not a diagnosis. What is true for one person is not necessarily true for another. Commonly, self-injury is dialogue with yourself – an expression of inexpressible emotion or an absence of self-value.
'They're manipulative'	Self-harm is a private activity. Accident and Emergency departments will see only a few of the injuries before healing: it's not about its effect on others.
'Self-harmers are usually hysterical women under 30 who grow out of it'	Recent research shows the difference in rate of self-injury between men and women in less marked. There is no evidence to show people 'grow out' of it. It is not a behaviour or development disorder'.
'It's self-inflicted so it's not serious'	How severe staff think the wound is won't tell them how bad the person feels. You may not witness all the forms of injury. Individuals have many ways of expressing their distress, often substituting one for another. Your perception of the seriousness of the injury may not indicate the extreme distress that injury represents.
'If you won't see a psychiatrist, you can't want to get better'	Psychiatry has had little success in helping individuals who self-injure; neither drug nor behavioural treatments can address the issue of self-worth.
'Either they enjoy pain or they can't feel it'	Each person has a different pain threshold. Commonly the loss of sensation some people experience during injuring returns soon after. By the time a person is receiving treatment, it is common for the sense of pain to be amplified.
'Don't waste your time with her, we've been treating her for years'	A long history of injury often results in being considered 'a hopeless case'. No attempt is made to offer support as it's assumed you're 'incurable'.
'It's tension-relieving'	Tension is rarely the sole pressure on an individual to injure: each person has their own pressure and triggers to injure.

Source: The National Self-Harm Network – www.nshn.co.uk. © Louise Pembroke, Andy Smith and the National Self-Harm Network.

The truth about self-harm

This article is for anyone who wants to understand self-harm among young people – why it happens, how to deal with it, and how to recover from what can become a very destructive cycle.

Understanding self-harm

Many find it almost impossible to understand why young people harm themselves, and how it could possibly help them to feel better. By deliberately hurting their bodies, young people often say they can change their state of mind so that they can cope better with 'other' pain they are feeling.

They may be using physical pain as a way of distracting themselves from emotional pain. Others are conscious of a sense of release. For some, especially those who feel emotionally scarred, it may be a way to 'wake up' in situations where they are so numb they can't feel anything. Overall, self-harm is a way of dealing with intense emotional pain.

Self-harm has a huge impact on the day-to-day life of those who do it. They will often try hard to keep what they're doing secret, and to hide their scars and bruises. But the burden of guilt and secrecy is difficult to carry.

It can affect everything from what they wear to the kinds of sports and physical activities they take part in, as well as close physical relationships with others, including sexual relationships.

Ultimately, because young people who do it are all too aware of the stigma of self-harm, it can affect their relationships with friends and family and their sense of self-worth.

Young people start self-harming to cope with their problems and feelings, but it very soon creates other serious problems. It can set up an addictive pattern of behaviour, from which it can be very hard to break free.

What is self-harm?

The phrase 'self-harm' is used to describe a range of things that people do to themselves in a deliberate and usually hidden way. It can involve:

⇨ cutting.

⇨ burning.

⇨ scalding.

⇨ banging or scratching one's own body.

⇨ breaking bones.

⇨ hair pulling.

⇨ swallowing poisonous substances or objects.

Who does it?

Research shows that one in 15 young people in Britain have harmed themselves. Another way of looking at it is that there are probably two young people in every secondary school classroom who have done it at some time. This means it's a very common problem.

Most young people who harm themselves are aged between 11 and 25. The age at which most people start is 12, but some children as young as seven have been known to do it.

> *Research shows that one in 15 young people in Britain have harmed themselves*

There is no such thing as a 'typical' young person who self-harms. About four times as many girls as boys do it. But it is also a serious problem among young men. Because they are more likely to do things like hitting themselves or breaking their own bones it can look as if they have had an accident, a fight or have been attacked.

Some very young children self-harm, and some adults too. Groups of people who are more vulnerable to self-harm than others include:

⇨ young people in residential settings like the armed forces, prison, sheltered housing or hostels and boarding schools.

⇨ lesbian, gay, bisexual and transgender young people.

⇨ young Asian women.

⇨ young people with learning disabilities.

'I felt a warm sense of relief, as though all the bad things about me were flowing out of me and it made me feel alive, real.'

Why do young people self-harm?

As one young person put it, many people self-harm to 'get out the hurt, anger and pain' caused by pressures in their lives. They harm themselves because they don't know what else to do and because they don't have, or don't feel they have, any other options.

For some young people, self-harm gives temporary relief

MENTAL HEALTH FOUNDATION

and a sense of control over their lives. But it brings its own very serious problems.

When asked about the issues that led them to self-harm, young people most often said it was linked with:

⇨ Being bullied at school.

⇨ Stress and worry about school work and exams.

⇨ Feeling isolated.

⇨ Not getting on with parents or other family members.

⇨ Parents getting divorced.

⇨ Bereavement.

⇨ Unwanted pregnancy.

⇨ Experience of abuse earlier in childhood.

⇨ Current abuse – physical, sexual or verbal.

⇨ The self-harm or suicide of someone close to them.

⇨ Problems to do with sexuality.

⇨ Problems to do with race, culture or religion.

⇨ Low self-esteem.

⇨ Feelings of rejection socially or within their families.

If you are being abused, it is vital that you get help. Please see the Mental Health Foundation website for details of organisations who can help.

'Some people do it for attention... that doesn't mean they should be ignored. There are plenty of ways to get attention, why cause yourself pain? And if someone's crying for help, you should give them it, not stand there and judge the way they're asking for it.'

Myths and stereotypes

There are lots of these attached to self-harm. This isn't surprising – myths and misunderstandings often arise when a problem is, like self-harm, poorly understood.

Negative stereotypes can be powerful. They need to be challenged because they stop young people from coming forward for help. They also mean that professionals, family and friends are much more likely to react in a hostile way to young people who self-harm.

Some of the most common stereotypes are that self-harm is about 'attention-seeking'. Most self-harm is actually done in secret for a long time and it can be very hard for young people to find enough courage to ask for help.

Self-harm is sometimes seen as a group activity – especially when young people are 'goths'. But it's very rarely a group activity.

Young people told the Inquiry that they couldn't say how many people they knew self-harmed, because no one wants to talk about it. The Inquiry could find no evidence to support the belief that this behaviour may be part of a particular youth sub-culture.

Is self-harm linked to suicide?

It is often the belief that self-harm is closely linked to suicide that frightens people most. But the vast majority of young people who self-harm are not trying to kill themselves – they are trying to cope with difficult feelings and circumstances. For many it is a way of staying alive.

Many people who commit suicide have self-harmed in the past, and this is one of the many reasons that self-harm must be taken very seriously.

How do people self-harm?

As shown earlier, there are lots of ways of self-harming. The most common is cutting yourself.

People who self-harm tend to go to great lengths to keep it secret. Young people can be hurting themselves over long periods of time without ever telling friends or family. They hardly ever seek medical attention or support.

Almost all self-harm is done in private, and on parts of the body that are not visible to others.

'People often link self-harm to suicide but for me it was something very different; it was my alternative to suicide; my way of coping even though sometimes I wished that my world would end!'

How does it start?

Many young people say that when they first harm themselves they believe it is a 'one-off' and that they won't do it again. But it doesn't solve the problems they are trying to cope with, and their difficult feelings soon come back again, leading them into a cycle of harming

MENTAL HEALTH FOUNDATION

themselves to try to cope.

Some young people have told us that they started to self-harm by accident – when they injured themselves accidentally and then started to cause themselves injuries on purpose to create the same feelings again.

Is it really addictive?

It is habit-forming, and some people believe you can become physically addicted to self-harm. There is evidence to show that chemicals, called 'endogenous opioids', are released when the body is injured in any way.

They are pleasurable and can make you less sensitive to pain. However, self-harm is not simply about chasing physical pleasure or relief through artificially stimulating a 'natural' reaction – it has to be understood for what it means to the young person who does it.

> *It is habit-forming, and some people believe you can become physically addicted to self-harm*

Often it is the way of coping or distracting yourself that is habit-forming. In other words, young people get used to it, and come to rely on it.

How do young people feel about harming themselves?

Young people who self-harm usually feel very guilty and ashamed of what they do, and do not want to talk about it. The stigma associated with self-harm is unhelpful, and stops people getting the support and information they need to find better and more helpful ways of coping.

What are the signs that someone is self-harming?

It is very difficult to tell whether someone is self-harming. One sign might be that they insist on covering up their bodies – even when it is warm.

They may avoid activities that involve showing themselves, such as swimming or games. Secretive behaviour, and wanting to be alone lots can also be a sign.

Many of the usual signs of emotional distress – becoming withdrawn, quiet, appearing 'washed out' and lacking energy – can also be signs that someone is self-harming.

'I feel a lot more confident. I've learned to be more open about my feelings and been able to move on. I felt that, without them knowing, I was being held back.

I've been able to come out of myself and explain what I do, and make sense of it, not keep having to lie and cover up what I did. I no longer feel ashamed as I know people are supporting me.'

How do I stop someone from self-harming?

It may be very difficult if someone you care about is self-harming, but trying to force them to stop doesn't work. It is very clear that self-harm in many cases is a pattern of behaviour that may have gone on for a long time, and most young people would find it virtually impossible to give up overnight, even if they wanted to.

Feeling in control is something that young people who self-harm say is very important to them. The good news is that being able to take control is one of the most important factors in the ability to recover from a pattern of self-harm, too. It is very important that the decision to stop comes from the person who is self-harming.

For many young people, stopping or reducing their self-harm is a long and slow process. Young people need the opportunity to build up their coping skills gradually, and may go on harming themselves for some time.

It can take time for young people to reach the point where they can start to give up. In the meantime, learning how to cause themselves the least possible damage can be crucial, and the first step in their journey to learning other ways to deal with difficult feelings. This is called 'harm reduction' and you can find out more about this from other organisations like Siari.

For most of the young people we spoke to, the recovery process began with tackling the underlying problems that were causing their self-harm. This sometimes involved counselling, sharing their problems, or tackling bullies. Helping a young person to tackle their underlying problems is something very useful you can do.

They also broke the habit by learning new coping strategies or using 'distraction techniques' when they felt the urge to hurt themselves. Different people need different distraction methods, and may need different things for different moods or situations.

Finding what is most helpful takes time, but young people who have persisted with it emphasise that trial and error will find something that works.

⇨ The above information is reprinted with kind permission from the Mental Health Foundation. Visit www.mentalhealth.org.uk for more information on this and other mental health issues.

© Mental Health Foundation

MENTAL HEALTH FOUNDATION

Coping tips and distractions

Information from TheSite.org

By Julia Pearlman

No one is going to tell you that it's easy to stop self-harming, especially when you're doing it because you see no other way out. But by finding alternatives, you may be able to reduce the urge to self-harm, as well as minimising the damage.

It may be that you've tried a number of alternatives to self-harming and they don't work – but perhaps there's something you've not tried, or it's just that you're not sure how best to do it. There are several ways you can cope with self-harming, whether it's by distracting yourself, or by finding a substitute for self-harm.

Is using an alternative as bad as self-harming itself?

Using alternatives to self-harm will help you get through an intense moment when you may feel a strong urge to hurt yourself. But it's never going to be easy, especially when you're trying to break the cycle for the first time.

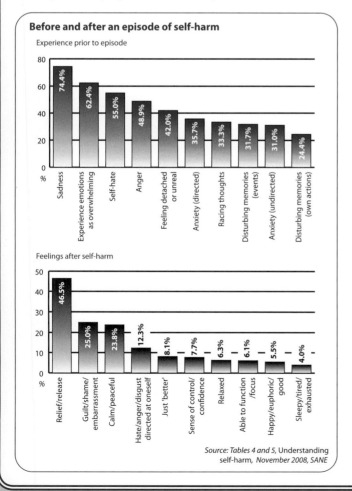

Before and after an episode of self-harm

Experience prior to episode

Sadness	74.4%
Experience emotions as overwhelming	62.4%
Self-hate	55.0%
Anger	48.9%
Feeling detached or unreal	42.0%
Anxiety (directed)	35.7%
Racing thoughts	33.3%
Disturbing memories (events)	31.7%
Anxiety (undirected)	31.0%
Disturbing memories (own actions)	24.4%

Feelings after self-harm

Relief/release	46.5%
Guilt/shame/embarrassment	25.0%
Calm/peaceful	23.8%
Hate/anger/disgust directed at oneself	12.3%
Just 'better'	8.1%
Sense of control/confidence	7.7%
Relaxed	6.3%
Able to function/focus	6.1%
Happy/euphoric/good	5.5%
Sleepy/tired/exhausted	4.0%

Source: Tables 4 and 5, Understanding self-harm, *November 2008, SANE*

Doing something like squeezing ice won't cure the roots of your distress, but it may help you to use a more productive coping mechanism and show you that you can cope with stress in a less harmful way. You'll have to make a conscious effort to not hurt yourself, but the important thing is that if you do decide to use an alternative, you've made that choice yourself.

> **'One of the reasons that young people say they self-harm and may be cutting or injuring themselves, is that something has happened in their life that has made them feel contaminated or polluted by what's happened'**

Minimise self-harm damage

If you feel an even stronger urge to self-harm, try the following harm minimisation tips:

⇨ Use a red felt tip pen to mark where you might usually cut.

⇨ Hit pillows or cushions, or have a good scream into a pillow or cushion to vent anger and frustration.

⇨ Rub ice across your skin where you might usually cut, or hold an ice-cube in the crook of your arm or leg.

⇨ Put elastic bands on wrists, arms or legs and flick them instead of cutting or hitting.

⇨ Have a cold bath or shower.

'One of the reasons that young people say they self-harm and may be cutting or injuring themselves, is that something has happened in their life that has made them feel contaminated or polluted by what's happened, whether it's physical or emotional,' says Frances McCann, mental health practitioner. 'It becomes a way of "letting something out" and dealing with feelings of self-disgust or low self-esteem.'

If you are going to harm yourself:

⇨ Avoid drugs and alcohol as these can lead you to do more damage than you intended.

⇨ Get your tetanus vaccination up-to-date.

⇨ Try to avoid doing it when in a highly distressed state as you may cause more damage than you intended.

⇨ Learn basic first aid.

⇨ Self-harm is private, but think about how you can quickly access help if you seriously hurt yourself.

THESITE.ORG

- ⇨ Avoid using tablets or medicines – there is no such thing as a safe overdose.

The A-Z of distractions

Often the best thing is to find out what has worked for other people who understand where you're coming from. TheSite.org asked young people from young people's mental health service, 42nd Street in Manchester, to come up with some of the alternatives that help them.

- ⇨ Alternative therapies: massage; reiki; meditation; acupuncture; aromatherapy.
- ⇨ Bake or cook something tasty.
- ⇨ Clean (and won't your folks/housemates be pleased!).
- ⇨ Craftwork: make things; draw or paint.
- ⇨ Dance your socks off.
- ⇨ Eat sweets or chocolate for an instant sugar rush (but be careful of the dip in your mood once it's over).
- ⇨ Exercise for a release of endorphins and that feel-good factor.
- ⇨ Forward planning – concentrate on something in the future, like a holiday.
- ⇨ Go for a walk (preferably further than the local pub).
- ⇨ Go online and look at websites that offer you advice and information.
- ⇨ Hang out with friends and family.
- ⇨ Have a bubble bath with lots of bath bombs fizzing around you.
- ⇨ Have a good cry.
- ⇨ Hug a soft toy.
- ⇨ Invite a friend round.
- ⇨ Join a gym or a club.
- ⇨ Knit (it's not just for old people you know).
- ⇨ Listen to music.
- ⇨ Moisturise.
- ⇨ Music: singing; playing instruments; listening to (basically making as much noise as you can).
- ⇨ Open up to a friend or family member about how you are feeling.
- ⇨ Pop bubble wrap.
- ⇨ Phone a helpline or a friend.
- ⇨ Play computer games.
- ⇨ Play with a stress ball or make one yourself.
- ⇨ Read a book.

- ⇨ Rip up a phone directory (does anyone actually use them these days?).
- ⇨ Scream into an empty room.
- ⇨ Shop till you drop.
- ⇨ Smoke – smokers find that having a fag can help.
- ⇨ Spend time with babies (when they're in a good mood).
- ⇨ Tell or listen to jokes.
- ⇨ Use the Internet.
- ⇨ Visit a zoo or a farm (animals do the best things).
- ⇨ Volunteer for an organisation (will make you feel all warm inside).
- ⇨ Watch TV or films – particularly comedies.
- ⇨ Write: diary, poems, a book.
- ⇨ Write negative feelings on paper, then rip them up.
- ⇨ Yoga: meditation, deep breathing – this might help you relax and control your urges.
- ⇨ Zzz – get a good night's sleep.

- ⇨ The above information is reprinted with kind permission from TheSite.org. Visit www.thesite.org for more information.

© TheSite.org

THESITE.ORG

Selina's story: 'I wanted to punish myself for being such a failure'

Selina Aktai, 39, from north London, cut herself almost constantly between the ages of 12 and 36.

There was a build-up of unhappiness from when I was really young. After my mum died when I was 12, my dad remarried really quickly and the whole family changed. I felt out of control, angry at my dad and completely alone. One day I was shaving my legs in the bathroom and I cut myself accidentally. Watching the blood trickle into the water made me feel so much better; it felt like a release. From then I started cutting my legs in secret, every other day, as a way to convey how I felt. I would cut until I could see blood and then cover them with plasters.

I never told anybody. We didn't do that in our family. We were taught to have good manners, to respect our parents and do well at school; not to talk about our thoughts and feelings. I was acting out at school, but everyone just thought I was difficult. No one asked me how I felt.

Even when I got my life together, settled down and got a job with the council, I still hurt myself at times, and the suicidal thoughts got stronger whenever I tried to resolve the difficulties with my family

After a few years I started to have suicidal thoughts and began to experiment with paracetamol; I wanted to see how far I could go. I was holding down a job, but then my Dad convinced me to get married in Bangladesh. It didn't work out, and I came home. I then spent five chaotic years travelling around the country, completely out of control, cutting myself and taking overdoses, but still I didn't tell anyone. Deep down, I knew I was taking risks with my life, but I didn't know any other way. By this stage cutting no longer made me feel better: I did it because I wanted to punish myself for being such a failure.

Even when I got my life together, settled down and got a job with the council, I still hurt myself at times, and the suicidal thoughts got stronger whenever I tried to resolve the difficulties with my family. It all came to a head eventually, and I made a plan to jump off Westminster Bridge. That's when I ended up in hospital in 2005.

Hospital is not the right place for people who self-harm. I got myself out and after six months got an appointment with a fantastic therapist – the first time I found someone who listened to me, understood my culture and helped me to express how I felt with words. I haven't hurt myself for many, many months and feel much more in control of my life. My family still has no idea about what I was doing and how bad things got.

This article first appeared in The Independent, *22 March 2009. It is an extract from a longer article entitled* Self-harm: A British disease.

© The Independent

Understanding self-harm

Summary and discussion.

SANE

Nearly 1,000 people, 827 of whom had first-hand experience of self-harm, took part in SANE's self-harm study, which started in 2005. Over 500 participants were still harming at the time of filling in the survey. The most commonly reported method was cutting/scratching (93%) or burning (28%) the skin and the most frequently targeted body parts were arms (83%) and thighs/legs (50%). A fifth had overdosed on medicines. It seemed to us that the majority of participants, when answering further questions about self-harm, were thinking mainly of cutting/scratching or burning. The functions and motives of overdosing seemed to differ slightly from those associated with cutting and burning.

Despite being thought of as something that teenagers and young adults do, the results from our survey show that self-harm affects people of all ages. The age range of those who were still harming at the time they took part was 12-59 years of age, and while some people were reporting that they had first started self-harming as young as four, others had not harmed until they were in their late fifties. Although the majority were female, just over 100 men who had at some time harmed themselves took part in the survey (this made up 12% of all participants who had harmed). It is still unclear whether self-harm really is that much more common in girls/women than in boys/men, or whether the former are just more willing to talk about it and seek help.

What motivates self-harm – and what does self-harm do?

Our survey results showed that each individual act of harm can have a number of meanings and motivations, and these may evolve as years go by.

Self-loathing and need for punishment

Self-loathing and a need to punish oneself were found to be significant factors in motivating self-harm right from the start; each was identified by well over a third of the participants as a contributing motive for their first act of self-harm and the proportion of participants reporting these motivations increased to 43% and 45% respectively for more recent acts. We also found that those who harmed most frequently (daily or weekly, rather than every few weeks or months) tended to report these motives for their recent acts of self-harm more often. The reason for this? We think it has to do with the fact that many participants tended to have a very negative view of their self-harm (not a surprise, given

how stigmatised the behaviour is). One in four reported feeling one of the negative social emotions of guilt, shame or embarrassment after acts of self-harm, and one in eight felt hateful towards, angry or disgusted with themselves afterwards. It is easy to see how this process can feed itself in a cycle of harm and self-recrimination, fuelled by stigmatisation and ill-informed prejudices of others. As counter-intuitive as it may seem, in many cases (and, as our findings suggest, especially for those who harm frequently) the best way to help someone to reduce their self-harm may be to help them to feel alright about it.

Key findings:

⇨ 55% of participants reported experiencing self-hate prior to harming.

⇨ 43% reported self-hate being a motive for self-harm.

⇨ 45% reported harming in order to punish themselves.

⇨ Those who harmed more frequently (daily or weekly, rather than every few weeks or months) were significantly more likely to be motivated by self-loathing or a need to punish themselves than those who harmed less frequently.

⇨ One in four participants reported feeling guilty, ashamed or embarrassed after an episode of self-harm.

Feeling too little or too much

One way of helping someone come to terms with their self-harm is to engage with their reasons and motivations for doing it. This is not always easy; many of our participants wrote about hiding their self-harm so that they wouldn't have to explain it to others, and the second most often cited reason for hiding self-harm was that family and friends would not understand. When it comes to the most frequently reported function of self-harm, emotion regulation, there seems to be an inherent difficulty in putting the experiences into words. This difficulty seemed to arise in two main kinds of experience. First, emotions are felt and recognised as, for example, sadness, anger, anxiety and so on – but the way in which emotions are felt is different: they are overwhelming, out of control, physically uncomfortable or confused. Alternatively, the person feels nothing: empty, dead, disconnected from the world and other people, and they feel as though they are struggling to maintain a coherent sense of self. These ways of feeling

SANE

are very hard to find language for, and the person who harms is often left with a feeling that only those who share such experiences (i.e. others who self-harm) can understand why they do it.

There are many aspects of this function of self-harm that are a mystery: it isn't known, for a start, why it should be that self-harm is capable of releasing anger, lifting depression and alleviating anxiety in some people. There is even a sense in which the function of self-harm is paradoxical; it appears that whilst self-harm can help someone to feel less, it can at other times help them to feel more. We are working on this question at the moment and hope to publish our findings soon. The last finding presented in the list below is also curious: why should it be that those who harm less frequently are more likely to do it in order to feel something, or to feel more real?

Key findings:

⇨ When asked how self-harm had helped them, 39% of participants wrote that it helped them regulate or release emotion.

⇨ 62% experienced overwhelming emotions before harming and 63% had harmed to relieve mental pain.

⇨ 34% had harmed in order to feel something.

⇨ 42% of participants felt detached or unreal before harming.

⇨ After harming, the positive effects felt most commonly were relief/release (47%) and sense of calm and peace (24%).

⇨ Those who harmed less frequently were more likely to cite 'wanting to feel something' or 'wanting to feel real' as a reason for their harm.

Secret self

Recognising that there was something different about their emotive experience, participants often expressed that there was something wrong about how they were feeling. This sense of inner life (feelings, thoughts, beliefs) being something incongruent with what is acceptable, something to feel bad about and to hide from others, was present in many guises throughout the participants' responses. When participants talked about the function of self-harm in their lives, they often mentioned that it helped them to keep their real feelings under wraps, to stop their anger or sadness 'spilling out'. There was a 'secret self' that had become separated from the 'social self', and participants worried about 'being found out' as someone who hates themself, is angry, anxious or depressed. This tendency to think of one's inner thoughts and feelings as unacceptable to others and as something to avoid showing in behaviour was found to be associated with a history of self-harm among the participants, and even more strongly, with current self-harm. Those who thought their inner lives least acceptable and most in need of hiding, also tended to be those who harmed most frequently. Given that the thoughts and feelings of the 'secret self' are not allowed to manifest in the physical, interpersonal world of expression and behaviour, it is little wonder that the fourth most frequently named function of self-harm was its ability to give mental distress a physical form, to make it tangible rather than the elusive experience it can be when it is refused its natural ground for playing itself out.

Key findings:

⇨ Feeling that your thoughts and feelings, if known by others, would be unacceptable to them was found to be associated with both current self-harm and a history of self-harm (and more strongly with the former).

⇨ Feeling unable to let your thoughts and feelings manifest in your behaviour was found to be associated with both current self-harm and a history of self-harm (and more strongly with the former).

⇨ Out of participants who were harming at the time of filling in the survey, those who thought their inner lives least acceptable and most in need of hiding tended to be those who harmed most frequently.

Control

The concept of 'control' is often mentioned in the context of self-harm. Over a third of our participants reported having harmed in order to feel in control. One of its possible meanings is emotion control. Another, behaviour control, was mentioned in the context of suppressing expression of thoughts and emotions in behaviour. Another form of behaviour control was also very important to the participants: over 100 participants

SANE

wrote about using self-harm to prevent suicide. This subject is discussed in more detail below, under the heading: 'Common misperceptions'.

In addition to the above-mentioned meanings for 'control', it seems that there is also something like a 'sense of control' that goes beyond emotion control and behaviour control, something that is part of our taken-for-granted experience, something nobody thinks about until it is suddenly gone. Self-harm can restore this feeling of being in control. Some participants connected this feeling with being able to function and focus, e.g. 'It helps me regain a sense of control and so enables me to get on with everyday things again.'

Key statistics:

⇨ One in three participants had at some point harmed in order to feel in control.

⇨ 17% used self-harm to control (rather than just release) emotions.

⇨ 28% used self-harm to control their behaviour.

Common misperceptions regarding motivations behind acts of self-harm

Sometimes self-harm can be used to take control of a situation – for example, one participant wrote about using self-harm to avoid physical punishment. However, our results suggest that these and other manipulative motivations for self-harm are rare. It has been a widespread misunderstanding about self-harm that its primary motivation is a manipulative one, e.g. attention-seeking. Several of the findings presented in this report indicate to the contrary: for one thing, the majority of those who self-harm apparently seek to hide it from their family (84%, n=692) and friends (66%, n=549). For another, the most important criterion for choosing a particular body part to harm was found to be ease of hiding the damage – this consideration often overrode a preference based on efficacy, for example. Further, only one in eight reported their first act of self-harm having been motivated by a desire to make others take notice or care, and this proportion fell to one in 12 for more recent acts.

Another common misperception about self-harm such as cutting or overdosing has been its identification with a failed suicide attempt. That self-harm is a risk factor for suicide is a well-documented fact to the point of being incontestable; Hawton et al. (2005) report that 25-50% of adolescents committing suicide have previously either engaged in self-harm or attempted suicide, and increased suicide risk has been shown in those who self-harm repeatedly. There is no doubt, then, that self-harmers experience more suicidal thoughts and feelings than those who do not harm. But this does not mean that when someone self-harms they intend to commit suicide. On the contrary: for most of the time

the majority of self-harmers do not want to die. Rather, they have persistent thoughts about death or suicide and the feelings associated with those thoughts, and they use self-harm to do away with them. Support for this claim comes from our study: over 100 participants stated that self-harm helped them prevent suicide. Once it is more widely known and understood that self-harm is primarily an act of self-preservation rather than destruction, and that self-harm plays a role in emotion regulation, this mistake is likely to be made less frequently.

Key findings:

⇨ Most of self-harm is hidden from others and motivated by private therapeutic needs rather than performed to achieve social or manipulative ends.

⇨ Although those who self-harm often feel suicidal when they harm, their intention is to seek relief from those feelings rather than to die. Self-harm is more an act of self-preservation, than it is an act of self-destruction.

November 2008

⇨ The above information is an extract from SANE's report *Understanding self-harm*, and is reprinted with permission. Visit www.sane.org.uk for more information.

© *SANE*

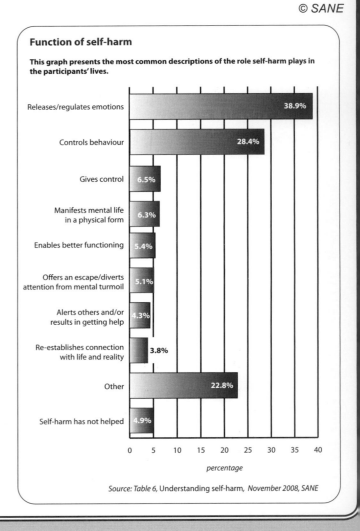

Function of self-harm

This graph presents the most common descriptions of the role self-harm plays in the participants' lives.

Function	percentage
Releases/regulates emotions	38.9%
Controls behaviour	28.4%
Gives control	6.5%
Manifests mental life in a physical form	6.3%
Enables better functioning	5.4%
Offers an escape/diverts attention from mental turmoil	5.1%
Alerts others and/or results in getting help	4.3%
Re-establishes connection with life and reality	3.8%
Other	22.8%
Self-harm has not helped	4.9%

Source: Table 6, Understanding self-harm, November 2008, SANE

SANE

What happens at A&E?

If you self-harm and need immediate medical assistance, your nearest Accident and Emergency (A&E) department is the first place to go to. TheSite.org finds out what happens when you go and how you should be treated.

Written by Chris Chapman and Dr Katie Muscroft

Each year, around 25,000 admissions to hospitals in England and Wales are made by young people who have self-harmed. All hospitals now have guidelines in place for dealing with young people who self-harm in order to make the environment as supportive and comfortable as possible. This means that when you arrive you should be given the same amount of respect, care and compassion as any patient.

Knowing when to go

If you need medical attention it's crucial to get yourself checked out. You can tend to some minor wounds yourself, but if you've hurt yourself badly, call an ambulance or make your way to the nearest hospital.

Self-harm in women's prisons

Information from the Ministry of Justice.

Although women make up only 5% of the total prison population, they account for almost half the self-harm incidents in prison. From September 2008 to August 2009, 47% of reported incidents of self-harm were by women. This involved 11,747 incidents. In 2008, 1,502 individual women self-harmed. This was a rate of 333 per 100,000 compared with a rate of 62 per 100,000 for men. The Corston report noted that 16% of women in prison self-harm compared with 3% of men.

In 2009, there were three self-inflicted deaths of women prisoners. This was a decrease from a peak of 14 in 2003. The Social Exclusion Unit's report noted that over a third (37%) of women sent to prison had attempted suicide before imprisonment.

July 2010

⇨ The above information is reprinted with kind permission from the Ministry of Justice. Visit www. justice.gov.uk for more information.

© Crown copyright

'If you've taken an overdose you should always go to the emergency department,' says Dr Katie Muscroft, who works in A&E. 'If you've cut yourself superficially (not fully penetrated the top layer of skin) give your wound a good clean with soapy water. If it's very deep, you feel it might need stitches or is bleeding excessively, go directly to A&E.'

The two most common forms of self-injury at A&E are cutting and overdosing – also referred to as 'self-poisoning'

Not every hospital has an A&E department; some hospitals have minor injury units that can deal with cuts and bruises, but usually wouldn't treat someone who came in by ambulance. You can find your nearest A&E department on the NHS website.

On arrival

The primary aim of an A&E is to ensure your physical injuries are dealt with as soon as possible. When you arrive, a 'triage' assessment will be made to determine how critical your physical injuries and state of mind are. These are categorised as 'minor' or 'major', with the most life-threatening prioritised. You'll either be directed to a bed or asked to wait in the waiting area.

Emergency treatments

The two most common forms of self-injury at A&E are cutting and overdosing – also referred to as 'self-poisoning'. Each case will be different, but the most likely emergency procedure for these is as follows:

Cutting

⇨ The doctor will ask what has happened, what you cut yourself with; when, where and why you did this.

⇨ You will be asked if you have a history of mental illness. As the physical injury is only one part of the emergency, this needs to be known so you can be suitably cared for.

⇨ Your wounds will be cleaned and the doctor will look to see how deep the cuts are and your muscles tested

MINISTRY OF JUSTICE / THESITE.ORG

for strength and nerves. If the wound isn't very deep and there doesn't seem to be any nerve or muscle damage, it can be closed with paper stitches or medical glue.

⇨ If the wound is particularly deep, a local anaesthetic to numb the area can be given.

Each year, around 25,000 admissions to hospitals in England and Wales are made by young people who have self-harmed

⇨ If there is damage to the nerves and muscles, you may be referred to a specialist, such as an orthopaedic surgeon or plastic surgeon. They may perform an operation, which is usually done the same or following day.

Self-poisoning and overdosing

Sometimes ambulance staff may need to give you treatment before you reach the emergency department. Depending on individual circumstances:

⇨ The doctor will need to know what you've taken, when you've taken it and how much.

⇨ Within an hour of taking the overdose you may be given a drink of 'activated charcoal' – a black, unpleasant-tasting drink that prevents the stomach from absorbing the poison.

⇨ Blood tests will be taken and paracetamol levels checked. It will depend on the amounts taken as to when you may be treated. If there's evidence to suggest a very large overdose, treatment will start immediately, otherwise they will wait to find out the levels.

⇨ A drip treatment may be given to you via a cannula (a plastic tube inserted into a vein in your arm) and may need to remain in place for up to 24 hours.

⇨ For some overdoses you may just need observation in the hospital, sometimes for up to 12 hours.

Talking to the doctor

Going to A&E may be the very first time someone else has seen the effects of your self-harm. There are several options the doctor can make before discharging you, but the most important thing is that they feel you aren't at risk of seriously harming yourself.

An important part of this process is assessing your mental and emotional state. This assessment may be done by a duty psychiatrist or psychiatric nurse. You should try and be honest about your feelings, including whether you have any suicidal thoughts.

'You should talk to someone about why you felt the need to cut yourself and if you want any help,' says Dr Muscroft. 'If a professional can help from the start, you can get the help you need as soon as possible.'

Unfortunately A&E doctors don't always have the time they would like to chat to a patient and not every hospital has a social worker or Community Psychiatric Nurse (CPN) for you to talk to either, but things are slowly improving. If this is the case, the hospital should try to make sure that you will be put in touch with someone who does have time to talk to you.

⇨ The above information is reprinted with kind permission from TheSite.org. For more information on this and other related topics, visit their website at www.thesite.org

© TheSite.org

New report highlights self-harm needs to be taken more seriously

17% of respondents identified as lesbian, gay or bisexual – over three times the national average – highlighting that urgent action is needed to support young LGBs.

By Joanne Dunning

A new report published today gives a rare insight into the behaviour and medical treatment of people who self-harm. Created by youth charities 42nd Street, Depaul UK and YouthNet, the report is an evaluation of 'Self-harm: Recovery, advice and support' a joint service provided on TheSite.org/selfharm.

It includes survey results with 179 users of the service, as well as excerpts of in-depth interviews with health professionals and young people – many of which are critical of NHS treatment of self-inflicted injuries.

> **The report found that of the 179 people surveyed, 17% described themselves as lesbian, gay or bisexual – over three times the national average (5%). This statistic highlights that self-harm is a serious issue amongst young LGBs which needs urgent attention**

The report highlights that self-harm needs to be taken more seriously by health professionals. One General Physician from a London A&E department is quoted in the reports as saying: 'If you go to A&E on a Friday night it is full of people who are sick. We are busy all the time, and maybe there is someone who self-harms who has come to A&E or called 999 but then they don't give us their history so you kind of just want to shake them and not waste our time because you have lots of people who are very sick.'

The report also includes user figures of the service and found that the article 'What happens at A&E?' was the third most used following 'What is self-harm?' and 'Why do people self-harm?' indicating that this is also an issue of concern to young people.

Alisia, 25, one of the young people interviewed in the report, spoke of her treatment: 'When I have been to hospital to get my wounds dressed I had horrible treatments from nurses. When I was in rehab I got horrible treatment because I was a self-harmer and the first rehab I was in they made me sign a contract to say if I self-harm I would get thrown out of the establishment.

'On the second rehab, because I was self-harming, they held a consultation group where people confront each other with their fears and anxieties. They sat everybody in a circle and the whole focus of the group was my self-harming and everybody was shouting at me, screamed at me, called me names, said that I was attention seeking. It did not help me at all it made me feel worse, made me want to self-harm more. It did not help at all.'

The report also found that of the 179 people surveyed, 17% described themselves as lesbian, gay or bisexual – over three times the national average (5%). This statistic highlights that self-harm is a serious issue amongst young LGBs which needs urgent attention.

LESBIAN AND GAY FOUNDATION

Ian Trafford, from the Manchester-based charity 42nd Street, who work with young people with mental health issues and have a specific LGB&T support group said: 'Self-harm is a hugely complex issue and is often linked to numerous emotional and mental health problems – when looking at the injury in isolation, it is easy to see why some people find it difficult to understand.

'However, it is disappointing that we're still hearing about examples of inadequate care for some young people following instances of self-harm. This is in spite of the fact that there are now NICE guidelines.

'In some areas, Manchester for example, the presence of mental health A&E liaison and crisis resolution teams has meant that young people are getting the treatment they need – a sign that with the right resources, training and understanding, things can be better for young people who self-harm.'

The report also found that despite the 'Self-harm: Recovery, advice and support' service being aimed at over-16s – 20% of respondents were under the age of 16, highlighting another area of need.

Between the launch of the online service in January 2009 and the end of May 2009, between 8,000 to 12,000 unique users visited TheSite.org/selfharm each month.

More than 83% of survey respondents found the self-harm section useful, and 80% said they would recommend the section to someone who needed advice or help about self-harm.

Patrick Daniels, Advice and Volunteer Manager for YouthNet, said: 'What's come through loud and clear from this report, and through our work with young people, is that providing the right kind of emotional and practical support to young people who self-harm at an early point can be life changing for them.

'Early intervention is proven to reduce the long-term impact of mental health and emotional issues for many, and the anonymity and accessibility of online services mean that the Internet service is perfectly placed to provide this support.'

Getting help

⇨ If you self-harm, or are worried about someone who does and want to know more about getting help visit: TheSite.org

⇨ LGF helpline: Alternatively, if you are feeling isolated, low, or just need someone to talk to, you can call the LGF helpline on 0845 3 30 30 30 (local call rate), 6pm-10pm (Staffed), 10pm-6pm (automated system).

⇨ Face 2 Face counselling sessions: The LGF's counselling service is currently able to offer free counselling to people under the age of 25. If you are thinking about coming out, or are struggling to accept your sexuality, maybe having problems with your relationship or are feeling anxious or depressed, whatever the reason, you may feel you might benefit from a period of counselling.

Self-harm is common amongst young lesbian, gay, bisexual and trans people, so much so that they have been identified as a particularly vulnerable group.

2 November 2009

⇨ The above information is reprinted with kind permission from the Lesbian and Gay Foundation (with thanks to YouthNet, who provided the contacts interviewed for this article). Visit www.lgf.org.uk and www.youthnet.org for more information.

© Lesbian and Gay Foundation 2010

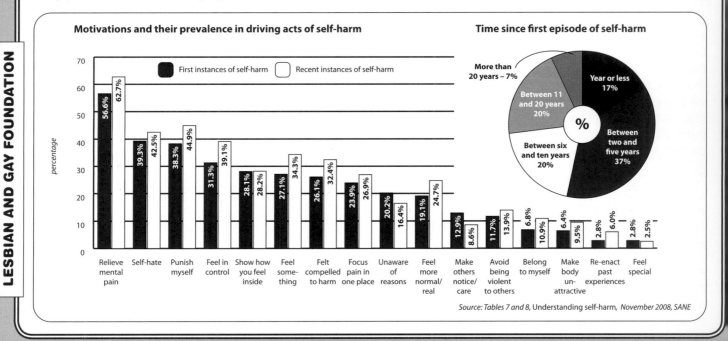

Source: Tables 7 and 8, Understanding self-harm, November 2008, SANE

LESBIAN AND GAY FOUNDATION

Self-harm makes its mark on pre-teens

Pupils aged as young as seven show scars of psychological distress.

By Adi Bloom

Self-harm tends to be associated with clichéd images of maudlin teenagers in darkened rooms. But primary school pupils also self-harm, according to recent research carried out by a child psychotherapist.

Linda Bean, who works for child and adolescent mental health services in north-east London, conducted detailed case studies of five children aged between seven and 11, all of whom self-harm.

Their methods ranged from cutting themselves with sharp objects to scratching or punching themselves and hitting parts of their bodies against a wall. Others were reckless with their health, failing to take prescribed medication or making themselves vomit. These methods are similar to those used by teenagers and adults. But unlike older self-harmers, young children often self-harm in public.

Ms Bean said: 'I believe this underlines its function as a communication to us. However, the children were ambivalent ... They (also) wanted to keep it secret in order to protect themselves from being let down and having the shame of others knowing they are needy.'

She found that the children shared an inability to manage their emotions and often felt overwhelmed by them. They saw emotions as treacherous, leading them into situations they had no confidence to cope with. Danielle described herself as modelling clay, rolled thinner and thinner until it broke apart.

Ah, to be young and without a care in the world...

The children found discussion of negative feelings particularly threatening, fearing what might happen if they expressed their emotions. Ania said she might 'become an alien or a monster' who could 'really hurt someone'.

Others feared they would never be able to stem the flow of emotions that resulted. Bill worried that, if he ever began to cry, his tears 'would fill up all the oceans of the world'. Eugene said: 'They (emotions) are like a grain of sand, but when I talk about it they get bigger and bigger.'

All the children had also witnessed their parents or carers losing control and hurting themselves or other people. 'Crucially, they learnt that unrestrained feelings could be catastrophic. both to themselves and to others,' said Ms Bean. 'This in turn fed their unhelpful belief that feelings can be dangerous.'

Self-harm, Ms Bean believes, cuts off these feelings before they overwhelm the child. It is a way of anticipating anxiety, stopping it short and keeping it contained.

Eugene said of his sad feelings: 'They are outside me. I don't want them unless they become happy.'

Instead, the children channelled their emotions into their bodies. For example, while talking to a school counsellor, Ania jumped up and hit her leg hard against the radiator. But she was unable to link the discussion and her actions. Instead, she explained that she had 'feelings in my tummy', and that hurting her leg made them better.

Ms Bean said: 'Like Ania, all the children found it hard to pause and think before acting, which is a prerequisite for successful mood and behaviour control.'

Also, because of bad experiences at home, they had not developed a habit of seeking adult help, relying instead on a repertoire of avoidance, repression and denial. Self-harm became a coping mechanism.

Primary children who self-harm are unlikely to trust adults. Teachers who suspect that a pupil is self-harming should therefore be careful to avoid expressing shock and horror as this merely reinforces negative expectations.

'While self-harming behaviour is alarming for adults, from the child's point of view it is just the tip of the iceberg,' said Ms Bean. 'What lies out of sight, in the private world of the family, is much more lonely, terrifying and dangerous.'

Linda Bean's research appears in the latest edition of *Counselling Children and Young People*: www.ccyp.co.uk

Published in The TES *on 9 January 2009*

⇨ Information from TES Connect. This article in full can be found on their website: www.tes.co.uk/article.aspx?storycode=6006960

© TES

NHS services 'failing to support people who self-harm'

Information from the Royal College of Psychiatrists.

Many people who harm themselves are failing to receive the help they need because of a 'patchy' provision of services across the UK and a lack of supervision and training of NHS staff, the Royal College of Psychiatrists (RCPsych) says.

In a new report, *Self-harm, suicide and risk: helping people who self-harm*, the RCPsych examines the current provision of care for people at risk from self-harm and suicide, and makes a series of recommendations to improve standards of care.

Self-harm is defined as an intentional act of self-poisoning or self-injury, and includes suicide attempts. While there has been a downward trend in the number of completed suicides in recent decades, the incidence of self-harm in the UK has continued to rise over the past 20 years. An estimated four in 1,000 people have self-harmed, and the rate of self-harm in the UK's young people is among the highest in Europe.

As part of the report, the RCPsych surveyed over 1,500 of its members. Less than half the respondents felt that they or their team had sufficient training to undertake assessments of people who had harmed themselves.

Many respondents reported that junior doctors and other inexperienced health professionals are left – often at night – to assess and manage the complex and potentially life-threatening situations of people who have harmed themselves or attempted suicide. The survey suggests the situation is particularly bad in Accident and Emergency departments.

Lord John Alderdice, who chaired the working group which produced the report, said: 'Our report highlights examples of excellent best practice, where dedicated staff are providing innovative, effective and humane services to people who harm themselves. However, overall the evidence painted a worrying picture of standards of care in UK hospitals. This situation is unacceptable by any reasonable standard. Lives may be at stake. Well-being certainly is.'

Lord Alderdice continued: 'When a person turns up to hospital having harmed themselves, this may well be the first time they have had contact with the health service. Failure to deal effectively with a person at this stage can have major repercussions. It may discourage them from returning in a later crisis and stop them getting the care they need. Experienced clinicians need to be involved from the outset, and psychiatrists need to be available to take a lead role in the process of helping people who harm themselves. I must emphasise that this is not because all of these people are suffering from mental illness, which is not the case, but because a sophisticated assessment is necessary to ensure the right management of the person and their problems.'

The report makes a series of key recommendations to improve the provision of services. Recommendations include:

⇨ NHS services, particularly in A&E, to be managed in a way which ensures people who have self-harmed or attempted suicide have proper access to care and treatment by fully-trained clinical staff, and that the NICE guideline on self-harm is implemented.

⇨ A change to the culture of NHS services, so that staff who encounter people who self-harm are trained and supported.

⇨ A proper public health strategy to cover self-harm, and for the suicide prevention strategy to remain a priority in all nations of the UK.

⇨ More funding of research on self-harm, which has been neglected and overlooked.

Joe Ferns, director of policy at Samaritans and member of the working group, said: 'This report is a timely reminder that good care for people at risk of self-harm and suicide can lead to a reduction in the nation's suicide rate. There is strong evidence of a link between economic hardship and suicide; figures released last week show that, in the Republic of Ireland, people taking their own lives in 2009 increased by 24 per cent, compared to the previous year.

'Meanwhile, 2008 UK figures showed the number of suicides and the suicide rate increased slightly compared to 2007. This could indicate the start of an upward trend continuing until there is an improvement in economic conditions. In the current economic climate, and against a backdrop of budget cuts, it is vital that the government is committed to a suicide prevention strategy.'

June 2010

⇨ Information from the Royal College of Psychiatrists. Visit www.rcpsych.ac.uk for more information.

© 2010 Royal College of Psychiatrists

Websites told to remove material promoting self-harm

Doctors call for policing of Internet as numbers admitted to hospital due to self-harm rise.

By Sarah Boseley

Doctors today called on websites to remove any material which romanticises or promotes self-harm by young people, as figures emerged suggesting a significant rise in the numbers admitted to hospital.

Around one in ten 11- to 25-year-olds – mainly but not only girls – will deliberately harm themselves at some point. According to the Centre for Suicide Research at Oxford University, admissions of under-25s who have damaged themselves deliberately with a sharp object have risen by 50% in five years, from 1,758 in 2004/5 to 2,727 in 2008/9.

'We are sure this is just the tip of the iceberg,' Professor Keith Hawton of the centre told the BBC. 'Pressures have increased and there's much more expected of young people.'

One in five young people questioned by the centre said they had first heard about self-harm from reading about it or watching a video online.

The Royal College of Psychiatrists says it is seriously concerned that some websites romanticise self-harm and may encourage young people to try it. It is calling for new curbs by website operators and moderators on self-harming content.

Dr Margaret Murphy, chair of the college's faculty of child and adolescent psychiatry, said the Internet anxieties follow concern about the growing mental health problems of young people.

'Unicef's report at the end of 2007 suggested young people in the UK were faring worse in terms of mental well-being than in other parts of Europe,' she told the *Guardian*.

Most self-harm involved cutting oneself, but from time to time young people burn themselves or bang their heads, she said. 'The reasons behind it are very complex but many young people who self-harm describe it as being a way of dealing with intolerable feelings and releasing or coping with them. They may feel self-loathing, self-hatred, shame, anger, frustration or sadness.' The triggers for these feelings include bullying, family conflicts, a sense of isolation and not fitting in, she said.

Videos featuring young people talking about their experiences of self-harm proliferate on the Internet, she said. 'Some of them are probably quite helpful – they help people feel they are not alone.'

But others have graphics, images and music and present self-harm in what could be an attractive light. 'I saw one of an American man who looked to be about 24 who decided to film himself in A&E where he had gone in and cut himself and he was sending it to his friends,' she said.

Sometimes the comments people post on films are not helpful. 'The anonymity means people will be harsher than they would in personal contact,' she said. This had also been a problem with websites where young people had discussed suicide, she added.

In a statement, the college called upon 'all website owners and moderators to ensure that material, images and commentary which appear to promote or romanticise self-harm are removed. We also call on them to ensure that any online content relating to self-harm is accompanied by information about relevant organisations which can offer advice and support. The Samaritans has issued guidelines for journalists on the responsible reporting and portrayal of suicide and self-harm, and we urge new media to adopt these guidelines as well.'

12 March 2010

© Guardian News and Media Limited 2010

THE GUARDIAN

Suicide

Information from NHS Choices.

Introduction

Suicide is the act of ending your life intentionally. The suicide rate in the UK has been falling since 1991, and in 2007 the rate was the lowest on record. There are more than 5,000 suicides in the UK each year.

Self-harm is the deliberate act of harming yourself, for example by overdosing on tablets or self-cutting. Sometimes, the intention of such acts is to die, and sometimes there are other motives, such as escaping from painful feelings or to release tension.

Self-harm is much more common than suicide. There are at least 140,000 attempted suicides each year in England and Wales.

Risk factors for suicide

There are many factors that can make a person more likely to end their life by suicide. For example, having a mental illness such as depression, or misusing drugs and alcohol.

The death rate from suicide is particularly high in men under 35.

Getting help

If you have had thoughts of suicide recently, or if you are feeling suicidal now, contact someone immediately for help:

⇨ See your GP or the out-of-hours GP service. If you have already taken an overdose or cut yourself badly, dial 999.

⇨ There are telephone helplines with specially trained volunteers who will listen to you, understand what you are going through, and help you through the immediate crisis.

⇨ Or you could contact a friend, family member or someone you trust.

The Samaritans operate a service that is open 24 hours a day, 365 days a year, for people who want to talk in confidence to someone about their distress, including self-destructive thoughts. Call 08457 909090.

Reasons for suicidal feelings

The reasons why someone may feel suicidal are often complex and may be linked to mental health conditions, such as depression. But there are things that make it more likely for you to have suicidal thoughts:

⇨ Something has happened in your life that has upset you. Perhaps you are being bullied, or you did not get the exam results you wanted. Perhaps you have split up with a partner, or someone close to you has died.

⇨ Your life has changed and you are finding it hard to cope with. Perhaps you have recently retired or your family has just left home. Perhaps you are having financial difficulties.

⇨ You have been drinking heavily or using illegal drugs.

⇨ Someone close to you has taken their own life.

⇨ You have depression or another mental illness.

Often, there is no single, clear reason why you are thinking about suicide. A run of small problems or bad luck, or simply a gradual build-up of hurt and pressure over time, can wear you down until you begin to have suicidal thoughts.

Most people who have thoughts of suicide do not really want to die, but suicide may seem the only way out from their problems or an end to the unhappiness they are feeling. In this state of mind it is often difficult to think clearly.

Who is at risk of suicide?

Some groups of people are known to be at particular risk of suicide because they have unique difficulties to face.

Older people

Until fairly recently, the suicide rate among the elderly was much higher than in other age groups, but now suicide rates in younger people are higher. Older people are particularly vulnerable because they are more likely to have to deal with the death of loved ones, to be lonely, and to have physical ill health.

Also, depression in older people may be overlooked in favour of treating the physical conditions that come with old age.

Other at-risk groups

Other groups at risk include:

⇨ People with serious mental health problems, such

NHS CHOICES

as severe depression, bipolar disorder (manic depression) or schizophrenia, particularly when they have recently been discharged from a psychiatric unit.

⇨ People with disabling or painful physical illnesses.

⇨ People who may feel isolated within society. Gay men and lesbians, students, the homeless, immigrants, old people and those in prison are at particular risk.

⇨ People who use illegal drugs or abuse alcohol. Alcohol and drugs affect reasoning, can act as a depressant, and can cause someone to lose their inhibitions, which makes them more likely to attempt suicide.

⇨ People who have suffered sexual or physical abuse.

⇨ People who have attempted suicide or self-harmed before.

Men and suicide

Men account for three-quarters of all suicides in the UK. Generally, men are more reluctant than women to talk about their feelings and to see their GP with psychological problems.

Suicide statistics

The suicide rate in the UK is continuing to fall and the 2007 figures are the lowest rate on record. However, the number of suicides is still a concern: in 2006, there were 5,554 suicides in adults aged 15 and over in the UK.

It is estimated that in England and Wales, at least 140,000 people go to hospital each year having attempted suicide.

Suicide and men

⇨ Three-quarters of suicides in the UK are by men.

⇨ Men aged 25-34 are at highest risk of suicide, followed by men aged 35-44.

⇨ Suicide is the second most common cause of death in men aged 15-44, after accidental death.

Suicide and young people

⇨ Suicide is the second most common cause of death in people aged 15-24, behind accidental death.

⇨ It is estimated that 7-14% of adolescents will self-harm at some point in their life.

Suicide and the elderly

⇨ In 2006, 217 people aged 80 or above took their own lives. This represents 5.2% of all deaths from suicide.

Suicide and mental illness

⇨ Research has shown that almost all people who end their life by suicide have a mental illness, most commonly depression.

⇨ About 10-15% of people with bipolar disorder will die by suicide.

⇨ About 4% of people with schizophrenia will die by suicide, often soon after their illness starts.

Preventing suicide

Depression is a common reason why someone may have thoughts of suicide, and most suicides are linked to depression in some way.

If you are feeling depressed or suicidal, it is important that you visit your GP. They can offer you a range of treatments, such as antidepressants or talking therapies, such as counselling or cognitive behavioural therapy (CBT).

Self-help advice

There are things you can do yourself that can help you fight thoughts of suicide as well as more general feelings of depression. They are intended to give you ways of coping with feelings of loneliness, unhappiness or sadness:

⇨ Try to remain connected with the world around you and avoid feelings of isolation. Talk to someone you trust about how you are feeling, and keep up with your friendships and interests, even though you might not feel like it at times.

⇨ Find things that will take your mind off negative thoughts. This might be making sure you are with people you like, taking a hot bath, doing some deep-breathing exercises, or treating yourself to some of your favourite food.

⇨ Try focusing on the good things you have done each day rather than the bad. It may help to imagine yourself in a happy situation, such as seeing your favourite band, meeting your favourite movie star, eating your favourite meal, or sunning yourself on a beach.

⇨ Exercise can stimulate your mind and body and help fight off depression. Daylight and sunshine can help put you in a brighter mood, so spend time outdoors. Make an effort not to go to bed until your normal bedtime and find things to do that give structure to your day, such as going for a walk each evening.

⇨ Avoid alcohol and illegal drugs. They may give you a lift at first, but they can make you feel even worse in the long run as large amounts of alcohol act as a depressant. Also, if you drink a lot of alcohol or have taken certain illegal drugs, you may make decisions that you would not normally make.

⇨ Join a self-help group. Meeting other people who are going through the same thing can be a great relief, and it can show you how other people have coped. Supporting others can make you feel better about yourself too.

NHS CHOICES

National suicide rates

The National Suicide Prevention Strategy was launched in 2002 with the aim of reducing the number of suicides in England by at least a fifth by 2010. The number of suicides each year is now falling, including suicides among young men and the elderly.

Getting help

If you have had suicidal thoughts recently, or if you are feeling suicidal now, you should contact someone for help. There are telephone helplines with specially trained volunteers who will listen to you, understand what you are going through, and help you through the immediate crisis.

Helplines

The Samaritans operate a service that is open 24 hours a day, 365 days a year. Call 08457 909090. If you prefer to write down how you are feeling, or if you are worried you might be overheard talking on the phone, you can email them at jo@samaritans.org

Childline runs a free helpline for children and young people in the UK. The call is free and the number will not show up on your phone bill. Call 0800 1111.

Talking to someone you trust

If you do not want to speak to someone on a helpline, you could contact:

⇨ a member of your family, a friend or someone you trust, such as a teacher;

⇨ your GP, a mental health professional or other healthcare professional; or

⇨ a minister, religious leader or someone in your community.

Talking to someone can help you see beyond feelings of loneliness or despair. It can help you realise that there are other options apart from ending your life.

Whoever you talk to, you should also visit your GP. They will be able to advise you on treatment if they think you are suffering from depression.

Helping someone else

If you are worried that someone you know might be depressed or having thoughts of suicide, you should look out for signs of change in their personality and behaviour. The signs to look for include:

⇨ losing interest in things they used to enjoy;

⇨ unhappiness;

⇨ lack of energy;

⇨ spending a lot of time on their own; or

⇨ a reluctance to spend time with other people.

If you see possible warning signs that someone you know may be thinking about suicide, it is a good idea to ask them 'Do you ever feel so bad that you think of suicide?' Do not worry that you might be planting the idea in someone's head. If they have been thinking of suicide, they will probably be relieved to talk about it and grateful that you are willing to be so open and understanding.

If someone confides in you, listen carefully to everything they say and try not to judge them. Sometimes just being there and showing that you care enough to listen can help. You should reassure them that others feel like this too and that they are not alone in trying to cope with suicidal thoughts. There are people who can help them.

If they will not talk to you, perhaps they would talk to a friend or a relative, or perhaps they would prefer to write down how they feel.

There are many factors that can make a person more likely to end their life by suicide. For example, having a mental illness such as depression, or misusing drugs and alcohol

---

You should always try to persuade someone to visit their GP if you think they might be suicidal or depressed.

It is important to look after your own health too. Knowing that someone you care about is feeling suicidal can be physically and emotionally draining. If you feel that this is too much to deal with by yourself, talk about it in confidence with someone you trust.

Helping your child

⇨ Notice when they seem upset, withdrawn or irritable.

⇨ Encourage them to talk about their worries, listen, and help them to find their own solutions.

⇨ Buy blister packs of medicine in small amounts. This helps to prevent impulsive suicides.

⇨ Keep all medicines locked away, including painkillers such as paracetamol.

⇨ Get professional help if family problems keep upsetting your child.

Source: RCPsych

February 2009

⇨ Reproduced by kind permission of the Department of Health.

© Crown copyright 2010 – nhs.uk

How to help someone who is suicidal

Information from Mind: www.mind.org.uk

Suicidal feelings are frightening for the person who is experiencing them and for partners, family, friends and colleagues. Anxiety and confusion about what to do and how to cope add to a distressing situation.

When are feelings 'suicidal'?

'Mum thought I should try for college. Dad just urged me to get any job. My sister called me a wimp for not travelling the world. My mates reckoned I should stick with our band; we'd make it big. My girlfriend nagged me to cut my hair and become a salesman. I used to bottle up my feelings. Who knows what I wanted? I just couldn't see the point of struggling on.'

Some people have a very strong, clear desire for death. They may feel hopeless about the future, believing that things will never get better. Suicide may seem to be the only way of solving problems, once and for all, and ending the emotional pain of living.

However, a lot of self-destructive emotion, thought and behaviour is far more confused than this. Someone who feels that their situation and problems have become intolerable may see no alternative but to attempt to kill themself. Yet, they are likely to have extremely mixed feelings about this, and feel very afraid.

Someone who tries to take an overdose of drugs, or to cut a vein in their wrist, may know only that they can't go on with life as it is. In the weeks beforehand, depression, hopelessness and irritability often build up their tension. Under pressure, people may become desperate, but may still feel confused. They may less want to die than to escape an impossible situation, to relieve an unbearable state of mind, or to convey desperate feelings to others. Many may be past caring whether they live or die. The important fact for others to recognise is that, however wavering and confused the feelings may be, they remain life threatening.

Self-harm is most common among young women, especially between the ages of 15 to 19

'Only when you know what it is like to feel depressed, to feel you are dying inside, can you know what it is like to be suicidal, to think that the whole dreadful, terrible, nagging, awful pain of it all might be swept away by a simple, single act of self-destruction.' Spike Milligan

Is self-harming behaviour suicidal?

'I'm writing to ask for help. I'm a Muslim girl and when I was ten I was badly abused by a family friend. I've never told anyone. Since then I've kept myself to myself and have tried to take overdoses of painkillers. Whenever I'm at home with the family, I'm scared and feel lonely. I'd like to leave my family and start afresh. I'm over 18. What should I do? At the moment I feel like doing something I should have done years ago – to stab myself.'

Self-harm is most common among young women, especially between the ages of 15 to 19. Some people who self-harm may also suffer from eating distress, and some may have been abused as children. Some hurt themselves – by cutting, burning or scratching – in order to cope with overwhelming emotions and to release tension, so that emotional distress is transformed into physical pain. They may have terrible feelings of guilt, shame and fear about what they are doing, and yet they may feel powerless to stop. People who deliberately harm themselves are not necessarily suicidal, however there is evidence of a link between attempted suicide and self-harming behaviour. Whether or not death is the objective, self-harm is not about seeking attention or playing games. Like suicidal feelings, self-harming

HELLO

MIND

behaviour may express a powerful sense of despair, and should be taken seriously.

Why do people become suicidal?

'When I grew up and things went particularly badly, I used to say to myself, over and over... "I wish I were dead". Then, one day, I understood what I was saying. I was walking along the edge of Hampstead Heath after some standard domestic squabble, and suddenly I heard the phrase for the first time. I stood still to attend to the words, repeated them slowly, listening, realising I meant it.'

The reasons why people become suicidal are a complex mix of personal and social factors. Hopeless and desperate feelings have many sources: a run of problems or bad luck may feel overwhelming; a sudden personal crisis may trigger despair; or despair may build slowly, as the pressures and hurts of many years wear down a person's self-esteem. Part of the picture may be a build up of unacknowledged anger that is turned inwards against the self. There may be a last straw – an incident or problem just before a suicide attempt – but this is often not the real cause. Just as a sense of despair takes years to build up, so suicidal feelings often develop gradually.

The greater the pain, the more a person needs to know that there is a way of stopping it. So, as life becomes more distressing and difficult to bear, the thought of death may grow more appealing. Personal beliefs about what death will bring – nothingness, a place in heaven, reunion with the dead, reincarnation – may bring comfort. People in a suicidal crisis often feel it's beyond their power to do anything about events and pressures in their life. When someone is feeling so helpless and hopeless, it may be comforting to think that death is still within his or her control.

Many people reach a stage in their life when they feel they can no longer cope or see any point in going on. These feelings are surprisingly common, but some groups of people appear particularly vulnerable to suicidal feelings.

Mental health problems

People with serious mental health problems, such as bipolar disorder (manic depression) or schizophrenia, have a considerably higher chance of dying by suicide than the general population (an increased risk of ten to 15 per cent, in the case of schizophrenia). Delusional ideas may contribute to suicidal thoughts (people may hear voices, for example, urging them to kill themselves), but this is not the most important factor. Lack of social support and a sense of hopelessness about the future is often what leads someone with a serious mental health problem to take their own life.

A study that looked at information about people who had died by suicide estimated that 70 per cent of recorded suicides were by people who experienced depression. Psychological factors and external situations and events may combine to drive someone to suicide. There seems to be a strong connection to recent, negative life events as well as to the onset of depression.

Alcohol and drug abuse

Misuse of alcohol and drugs increases the risk of suicide, especially in young men. These difficulties may already reflect painful, traumatic experiences, such as sexual abuse and early bereavement.

Social factors

Attempted suicide is much higher amongst the unemployed than amongst people who are in work. This is also true of homeless people. Young gay men and lesbians are particularly at risk too, possibly because of the discrimination they face in our society.

Sexual and physical abuse

A history of physical or sexual abuse puts young people at increased risk of suicide or deliberate self-harm. A violent home life is also likely to contribute.

Relationships and marriage

Relationship problems, especially disturbed family relationships, are often in the background when someone attempts suicide. It is often the case that a serious argument with a partner took place just before a suicide attempt. Social isolation, for men in particular, can play a big part. Being married seems to reduce a man's chances of dying by suicide. Men who are divorced, separated or widowed are among the most likely to kill themselves. Marriage doesn't seem to have the same effect on suicide rates among women. (Married women and single men are at the greatest risk of mental health problems.)

Gender

Men are more likely to take their own lives than women. The highest rate of male suicide since 1977 has been in those aged 15-44 years. The female to male ratio for suicides is about 1:3. For young people the ratio is about 1:4. The reason for this is not certain. It may be partly because men are much less inclined to be open about their feelings. Women tend to talk more about their problems, and may therefore get help more often.

Health problems

If someone has a long-standing or painful physical problem, they may become depressed, and this, in turn, makes them more prone to suicidal feelings. It's therefore very important that carers and professionals should be aware of this.

MIND

Prisoners

The suicide rate for men in prison is five times the total male suicide rate. Many teenagers are traumatised by conditions in custody, where bullying is rife. However, the highest number of suicides in 2002 was in the 30- to 39-year-old age group.

Occupation

Doctors, nurses, pharmacists, vets and farmers have a higher risk than other professions. It's likely that this is connected to high stress, combined with easy access to the means of dying by suicide.

How do I know if someone close to me is suicidal?

'Some time ago, the young son of my friends died by suicide. His parents are beside themselves with grief. They live with that terrible helplessness that comes from feeling that there was a soul so troubled, but perhaps so self-contained, that no one knew.'

A suicide attempt can seem to come out of the blue, and family and friends may feel mystified about why someone has taken their own life. But suicidal feelings often develop gradually, without others being aware of them. Often, people find it hard to talk about these forbidden feelings and therefore disguise them.

Warning signs

⇨ feelings of failure, loss of self-esteem, isolation and hopelessness.

⇨ sleep problems, particularly waking up early.

⇨ a sense of uselessness and futility. Feeling 'What's the point?'

⇨ taking less care of themselves; for example, eating badly or not caring what they look like.

⇨ suddenly making out a will or taking out life insurance.

⇨ talking about suicide. It's a myth that people who talk about suicide don't go through with it. In fact, most people who have taken their own lives have spoken about it to someone.

⇨ a marked change of behaviour. Someone may appear to be calm and at peace for the first time or, more usually, may be withdrawn and have difficulty communicating.

There is a particular risk of suicide when someone who has been suffering from depression is just beginning to recover. They may have the energy to kill themselves that they lacked when they were severely depressed.

Someone who has thought about suicide in the past, however vaguely or rarely, is more likely to resort to it as a means of coping when life becomes stressful.

'One becomes trapped in a situation, stepping into another world with them, yet because you love them, you can't let go of the hope that they will change back to the person they were... They hold something of you in their hands... and if they were to go down, they take part of you with them. So, you have to protect them in order to protect yourself.'

Don't people have a right to kill themselves, if they want to?

'A part of me always knew he was dying, even though his body remained alive despite eight suicide attempts. The agony he experienced had caused a kind of death inside, already, and however much he struggled to believe that life could win through, ultimately it could not and he made his choice accordingly.'

Some people make repeated suicide attempts and appear to express a strong, unwavering wish for death. One carer's reaction on being told of her son's death was, 'Thank goodness for that'. Family and friends may come to accept that death is the inevitable outcome of so much emotional anguish. They may feel relieved that the person will not have to face further suffering. Those who have attempted suicide before have a higher chance of eventually dying by suicide, although many people have suicidal feelings without acting on them. Suicidal feelings may come and go according to the stresses and strains in day-to-day life.

Even when someone appears to be absolutely determined to take their own life, the importance of talking and examining every possible option and source of support can't be overestimated. Encourage the person not to view suicide as the only solution, and to see there is another way of resolving problems.

How can I help someone who feels that bad?

'After he made the first two suicide attempts in the space of 24 hours, I felt completely wiped out. I felt, overwhelmingly, that it must be so awful being married to me, he'd rather be dead.'

If you are trying to help someone who is suicidal, your chief concern will be their immediate safety and the causes of their desperation. It's important to encourage the person to talk about their despairing feelings.

Don't dismiss expressions of hopelessness as a 'cry for help' or try to jolly them out of it. Talking openly about the possibility of suicide will not make it more likely to happen. Just being there for the person and listening in an accepting way can help them feel less isolated and frightened.

It may be useful to emphasise to the suicidal person that suicide may not be the quick answer they are

MIND

hoping for. Indeed, an attempt may fail and result in greater suffering, such as severe disablement or brain damage.

Persuade them to get help

It's important to persuade someone who is feeling suicidal to get some outside support. Their GP is a good starting-point. He or she can arrange for the person to get professional help, such as psychotherapy or counselling, and may prescribe antidepressants, if appropriate.

There are organisations, such as Samaritans, that offer emergency helplines for people who are feeling desperate. They may also offer ongoing support in the form of self-help groups, general advice and information.

It's a good idea to discuss strategies for seeking help if the person has suicidal thoughts. Creating a personal support list is a useful way of reviewing every conceivable option. The list may include the names, phone numbers and addresses of individuals, helplines, organisations and professionals available for support. Persuade the person to keep this list by the phone and to agree to call someone when they are feeling suicidal. For a young person who has expressed suicidal feelings, drawing up such a list is, in itself, a sign of care and concern. Often, young people may resist sharing their personal feelings and problems. If they are reluctant to seek outside help, the information may provide food for thought, allowing them the option when ready.

In an emergency

If you feel someone is in real danger of suicide, has a mental health problem and will not approach anyone for help, you may think about contacting social services. Under the Mental Health Act 1983, a person can be treated without their consent. This is, inevitably, a heavy responsibility.

Addressing the underlying problems

Surviving or diffusing a suicidal crisis is one thing; solving the underlying problems is another. The difficulties that nurture despair are usually complex and don't vanish quickly. It's essential to address them, however, or suicidal feelings may well return.

Look after yourself

If you are in a close relationship with someone who has suicidal thoughts, you are likely to feel fearful, angry or guilty. You will need to find someone – whether a friend, family member, a professional, or a carers' support group – in whom you can confide. Compile your own support list.

⇨ The above information is reprinted from the Mind booklet *How to help someone who is suicidal* © Mind 2008. Visit www.mind.org.uk for more booklets on a wide range of mental health topics.

© Mind

Suicide in Scotland: key points

Information from the Scottish Public Health Observatory.

⇨ There were 843 deaths by suicide in Scotland in 2008 (deaths from intentional self harm and events of undetermined intent). This equates to an age-standardised rate of 16.1 per 100,000 population.

⇨ Based on three-year rolling averages there was a 10% fall in suicide rates between 2000-02 and 2006-08, although rates in men have increased slightly between 2005-07 and 2006-08.

⇨ In 2008, the suicide rate for males was over three times that for females.

⇨ Suicide is a leading cause of mortality in those under the age of 35 years.

⇨ Suicide rates increased with increasing deprivation with rates in the most deprived 30% of areas of Scotland significantly higher than the rate for Scotland generally.

⇨ Scottish rates vary across health board and local authority areas.

⇨ Between 1999-03 and 2004-08, the age-standardised suicide rate per 100,000 decreased in 13 of the 14 NHS Boards and in 26 of the 32 local authorities. The age-standardised suicide rate was significantly higher than the rate for Scotland in one NHS board and one local authority area.

⇨ Scotland's suicide rate is higher than rates in other parts of the UK.

⇨ Choose Life – Scotland's national suicide prevention strategy and action plan – was launched in December 2002. The ten-year strategy identifies key objectives and target groups for action.

August 2009

⇨ The above information is reprinted with kind permission from the Scottish Public Health Observatory. Visit www.scotpho.org.uk for more information.

© Scottish Public Health Observatory

MIND / SCOTTISH PUBLIC HEALTH OBSERVATORY

Suicide myths

Information from See Me Scotland.

Myth: Talking about suicide or asking someone if they feel suicidal will encourage suicide attempts

Serious talk about suicide does not create or increase risk, it reduces it. The best way to identify the possibility of suicide is to ask directly. Openly discussing someone's thoughts of suicide can be a source of relief for them and can be key to preventing the immediate danger of suicide.

Myth: Young people who talk about suicide never attempt or complete suicide

People who feel suicidal often talk about their feelings and plans to friends or others. Listening to, validating, and acting to support a person in this circumstance can save lives.

Myth: Suicide is illegal

Suicide is not illegal. Even so, there are still legal questions in the UK, where suicidal individuals have been charged with Breach of the Peace, and even been made the subject of Anti-Social Behaviour Orders. 'A woman who has attempted suicide four times has been banned from jumping into rivers, canals or onto railway lines.' (BBC, February 2005)

Myth: The only effective ways to help suicidal people come from professional therapists with extensive experience in this area

You can help by identifying the potentially suicidal person and talking to them about it. Preventing suicide is everyone's business.

Myth: If somebody wants to take their life, they will, and there is nothing anyone can do about it

Most people contemplating suicide do not want to die; they just want to stop the pain and difficulties they are experiencing. Although there are some occasions when nobody could have predicted a suicide, or intervened, in most cases there will have been a point in the process where a timely intervention might have averted the tragic outcome.

Myth: People who try to kill themselves must be mentally ill

Most people have clear reasons for their suicidal feelings. Most people have thought of suicide from time to time. Though suicide is the tragic consequence of many mental health problems, around three out of four people who take their own lives have not been in contact with mental health services in the year before their death.

Myth: Some people are always suicidal

Some groups, sub-cultures or ages are particularly associated with suicide. Whilst some groups seem to be at risk, such as young men, suicide can affect anybody. Many people think about suicide in passing at some time or another. There isn't a 'type' for suicide, and whilst there are warning signs, they aren't always there. Whilst there is a risk of further suicide attempts, people who have had suicidal feelings or have made an attempt on their life move on.

Myth: Suicide is painless

Most methods of suicide are extremely unpleasant. Some methods are violent, and catastrophic. Others are physically painful, and drawn out.

Myth: A suicide in the elderly is less of a tragedy than the suicide of a teenager

Any suicide is a tragedy for the individual, and the people around them. Saying 'at least they had had a good life' marginalises the grief of those left behind after a suicide in later life.

Myth: When a suicidal person begins to feel better, the danger is over

Often the risk of suicide can be greatest as depression lifts, or as after a person appears to calm after a period of turmoil. This can be because once a decision to attempt suicide is made people may feel they have a solution; however desperate it might be.

Myth: People who attempt suicide are merely looking for attention

Often people who attempt suicide do not want to die. When a person decides to make an attempt on their life, it is often because all other options, including the means to communicate with other people more conventionally are obscured by the pain they feel.

Myth: Those around someone who has had a bereavement by suicide shouldn't talk about it

Ignoring loss is denying loss. It should not be given 'the silent treatment'.

⇨ The above information is reprinted with kind permission from See Me Scotland. Visit www.seemescotland.org.uk for more information.

© See Me Scotland

SEE ME SCOTLAND

Suicide: young men at risk

Men are nearly three times more likely to take their own life than women. Among men under the age of 35, suicide is the second most common cause of death.

One of the reasons more men than women commit suicide is because many men are reluctant to talk about their feelings or to seek help when they need it.

Many men feel that they're expected to cope with problems themselves and that society puts pressure on them to conform to this idea of maleness. Being open about emotional problems is seen by some men as a weakness for which they'd be teased or ridiculed.

Suicide survivor Jude Redmond, 39, from Brighton, says he could not have discussed his depression with his male friends.

'My social life revolved around meeting friends in the pub,' he says. 'Our sense of humour is based on winding people up and finding a chink in their armour.'

Strong and silent

This idea of maleness is communicated to boys at a young age. 'The phrase "boys don't cry" is still used by some people today,' says psychotherapist Lucy Beresford.

'Mothers want to raise strong boys. There's a belief that girls can cry, but little boys' tears should be hushed up.'

But by keeping quiet, issues can take on an exaggerated importance in your mind and further deepen your anxiety.

'If you can't talk about a problem, it's very hard to put it into perspective, and problems can grow out of proportion in your mind,' says Jane Powell, director of the Campaign Against Living Miserably (CALM).

'There's a stereotype that men are supposed to be the strong and silent type. It's a stereotype which is reinforced daily across society,' she says. 'Discussing personal issues and how they feel is particularly hard for them.

'They are reluctant to talk to anyone about issues which affect them, including their wives, and certainly won't talk to their GPs.'

Practical help

CALM was founded in response to the high suicide rate among men aged 15 to 35. It has a website and a helpline, and has plans to launch a text and online support service.

'CALM is there to give support and practical information and advice,' says Powell. 'We know that men don't just want support, but they want practical help with their problems.'

Jude didn't get professional help. 'I thought I'd be alright,' he says. 'By the time I realised I needed help, I thought it was too late for anyone to help me.'

Biology

Women on the other hand feel a sense of physical release from sharing their emotions, according to Lucy Beresford.

'Men just don't feel that,' she says. 'They physically don't feel comfortable talking about their emotions.'

She says it's due to biology. 'When women are under pressure, talking about it and expressing their feelings releases the hormone oxytocin, which makes them feel better,' she says.

'Men don't get that response. Their levels of oxytocin are lower so they don't get the same sense of release.'

Cary Cooper, Professor of Organisational Psychology and Health at Lancaster University, agrees. He says men tend to have a lower EQ (emotional intelligence) than women.

'Men may be less able to talk about their feelings, express emotion or seek emotional support when they need it,' he says.

Nurture versus nature

The way many men cope with problems is to avoid or ignore them, often going to the pub with their mates to 'drown their sorrows'.

'If you feel there's nowhere else to go and you bury your feelings, the problems can accelerate and you can feel you have no control over events with feelings of hopelessness,' says Professor Cooper.

'But what you need to do is speak to someone who understands what you're going through, who can listen and help you go through your options for dealing with the problem.'

Professor Cooper says gender roles are increasingly blurred and it's becoming acceptable for men to express emotion.

'We have more male role models expressing emotion and society is slowly moving in that direction,' he says.

Reviewed 5 December 2008

⇨ Reproduced by kind permission of the Department of Health.

© Crown copyright 2010 – nhs.uk

NHS CHOICES

Warning signs of suicidal behaviour

Information from Console.

The best way to prevent suicide is through education and awareness. Most suicides are related to depression and, since we cannot always prevent depression, although we can frequently treat it successfully, we must learn to recognise these symptoms that may occur in ourselves or others.

Symptoms of depression

⇨ Depressed mood.

⇨ Loss of interest and enjoyment.

⇨ Reduced energy, being easily fatigued, diminished activity.

⇨ Marked tiredness on slight effort.

⇨ Reduced concentration and attention on a task.

⇨ Reduced confidence and self-esteem.

⇨ Feeling of guilt and unworthiness.

⇨ Bleak and pessimistic views of the future.

⇨ Ideas of acts of self-destruction or suicide.

⇨ Disturbed sleep.

⇨ Diminished appetite and libido.

⇨ Unexplained physical symptoms.

(Source: International Classification of Diseases, WHO [1992])

When should a person consult a doctor?

⇨ If symptoms as stated above persist for at least two weeks.

⇨ If normal stresses of life do not explain the symptoms.

⇨ When rest and relaxation have not helped.

What a person who feels suicidal may say

Direct messages include statements such as 'I am going to commit suicide,' or 'I don't want to live any more.' Indirect messages include statements such as 'Life isn't worth living,' 'I want to go to sleep and never wake up,' 'Soon it won't matter anymore,' and 'Do you think suicide is wrong?' These are subtler ways that people express their pain, hopelessness and possible suicidal thoughts.

How a person who feels suicidal may behave

Each of the following behaviours by itself may not signal suicidal thinking or depression, yet if several are present, there could be cause for serious concern.

⇨ Depression, moodiness, sadness, or lack of energy.

⇨ Talking directly or indirectly about dying or committing suicide.

⇨ Changes in sleeping habits (too much, too little).

The best way to prevent suicide is through education and awareness

⇨ Changes in eating habits (sudden weight gain, weight loss).

⇨ Discouragement about the future, self-criticism.

⇨ Recent lack of concern about physical appearance, hygiene.

⇨ Withdrawal from social contacts or communication difficulty.

DEPRESSION

CONSOLE

- Giving away prized possessions.

- Drop in school grades or work performance.

- Acquiring the means for suicide (guns, drugs, rope).

- Making final arrangements, writing a will.

- Taking unusual risks.

- Increased drug or alcohol use.

- Preoccupation with death through poetry and/or artwork.

- Previous suicide attempts (80% of those who kill themselves have attempted it before).

What may have happened to a person to arouse suicidal feelings?

The following events frequently lead to crisis. For some people, internal and external resources are present in sufficient amounts to cope. For others, intense feelings coupled with a lack of external resources result in serious emotional crisis.

- End of a serious relationship.

- Loss of a loved one to suicide.

- Death of a loved one.

- Divorce.

- Loss of a job.

- Financial difficulties.

- Moving to a new location.

- Isolation.

What can we do to help the person who feels suicidal?

- Show that you really care.

- Be non-judgmental (don't act appalled or offended).

- Talk openly about suicide by asking questions such as: 'Do you ever feel so bad that you think of suicide?' 'Do you have a plan?'(the more specific, the higher the risk) 'Do you know when you would do it (today, next week)?' 'Do you have access to what you would use?'

- Never keep a plan for suicide a secret.

- Ask if they have made prior attempts or are bereaved through suicide (again, this denotes higher risk).

- If risk seems high, stay with the suicidal person or ask someone else to stay with him or her until the crisis has passes or until help arrives.

- Help the suicidal to get help. It may be necessary to get the suicidal person to a GP or to a hospital

as soon as possible. Other resources may include informed clergy, psychiatrists, clinical psychologists, counsellors, support groups, supportive family members and select friends.

Most suicides are related to depression and, since we cannot always prevent depression, although we can frequently treat it successfully, we must learn to recognise these symptoms that may occur in ourselves or others

- The importance of continuing care and concern: just prior to suicide many depressed people continually apologise to anyone they think they have offended. They then take their own lives. Half the people who kill themselves do so within 90 days after the precipitating crisis. Hence the need for continued care and concern.

- The above information is reprinted with kind permission from Console. Visit www.console.ie for more information.

© Console

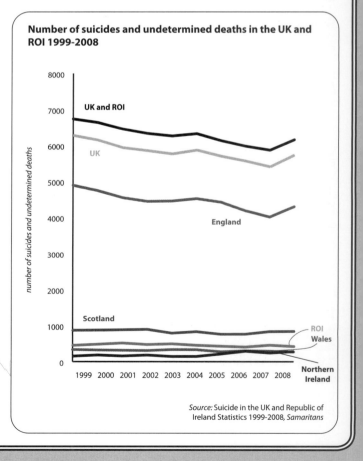

Number of suicides and undetermined deaths in the UK and ROI 1999-2008

Source: Suicide in the UK and Republic of Ireland Statistics 1999-2008, *Samaritans*

Understanding and preventing suicide in young people

What makes young people want to commit suicide, and, crucially, how can we prevent it?

By Jenni Whitehead

In the aftermath of the suicides of young people in Bridgend, Wales, where 19 young people under the age of 27 have hanged themselves, a suicide prevention project is to be set up using nearly one million pounds of lottery funding. Quite separately, the Samaritans is in the early stages of developing a suicide and self-harm response kit for schools, and has opened a consultation process to which anyone with relevant experience can contribute.

It is difficult to understand why a young person commits suicide, but the most recent statistics suggest that in the UK, more than 600 young people die by suicide each year. Suicide attempts don't make headlines, but their scale is noted in research on the Samaritans website: 'A conservative estimate is that there are 24,000 cases of attempted suicide by adolescents (10-19 years) each year in England and Wales, which is one attempt every 20 minutes (Hawton et al, 1999b).'

How can education staff help?

Professionals and particularly school-based staff need to be aware of signs and indicators of deep depression and suicidal thoughts and how to help young people cope and seek help.

Depression and other problems can manifest themselves from early childhood onwards: research estimates that one in five children have psychological problems. Acute mental illnesses such as schizophrenia and bipolar disorder often begin during the later teenage years. Although, thankfully, suicide is a rare occurrence, episodes of self-harm and/or suicidal behaviour are not – research suggests that one in ten among 15- to 16-year-olds in the UK and Ireland have self-harmed.

Early intervention can prevent situations from escalating and schools are ideally placed to both recognise children and young people at risk and offer support in-house and through involvement with external agencies. To this end, the Samaritans have produced a flexible teaching resource called DEAL (Developing Emotional Awareness and Learning), for use with 14- to 16-year-olds, which can be downloaded from the Samaritans' website. Many of their branches also offer talks in schools: to students, staff or parents.

Factors in suicidal feelings

The children's charity ChildLine, run by the NSPCC, has recently published research, *Saving Young Lives*, that draws on information from calls to their helpline during the course of one year.

Suicide was recorded by ChildLine counsellors as an additional risk when the following were noted as the main problem: bullying (337), sexual abuse (277), physical abuse (231), self-harm (27), eating disorder (18).

Behaviours and situations that could indicate risk of suicide in young people

The following list is offered as a guide and not as a diagnostic tool. Many of the behaviours given here are indicators that something is wrong and suicidal thoughts might not be the only issue:

⇨ change in sleeping or eating habits.

⇨ violent or rebellious behaviour, or running away.

⇨ drinking to excess or misusing drugs.

⇨ feelings of boredom, restlessness, self-hatred.

⇨ failing to take care of personal appearance.

⇨ withdrawal from friends, family and usual interests.

⇨ complaints about headaches, stomach aches, tiredness or other.

⇨ physical symptoms.

⇨ unresolved feelings of grief following the loss of an important person or pet (including idols such as pop stars and other 'heroes').

⇨ self-harm.

⇨ talking about methods of suicide.

⇨ dwelling on insoluble problems.

⇨ giving away possessions.

⇨ hints that 'I won't be around' or 'I won't cause you any more trouble'.

⇨ becoming over-cheerful after a time of depression.

On top of this, research suggests that certain situations put young people at more risk of suicide. These include:

⇨ loss, bereavement or the break-up of a relationship.

TEACHINGEXPERTISE

⇨ living in an isolated rural area.

⇨ going to prison.

⇨ the experience of racism or a culture clash.

⇨ struggling with sexual identity.

⇨ a history of suicide in the family.

⇨ illness or disablement.

⇨ previous suicide attempts.

⇨ unhappy circumstances at work, school or home, including bullying.

⇨ fear of underachievement.

⇨ a combination of any of the above.

Gender issues

The *Saving Young Lives* report describes massive gender differences. Young women attempt suicide four times as often as young men, but around four times as many young men die of suicide.

Suicide was recorded by ChildLine counsellors as an additional risk when the following were noted as the main problem: bullying (337), sexual abuse (277), physical abuse (231), self-harm (27), eating disorder (18)

Most of the research about suicide recognises the higher risk of death by suicide for young men but this can lead to a misconception that young women are less likely to attempt it, which may cause less attention being given to them.

ChildLine also reports that four times more girls than boys call ChildLine, suggesting that girls are much more likely than boys to seek help through talking to someone. Samaritans' research reveals that over 60% of teenage boys don't know what to do when someone becomes emotional towards them, over 40% of girls don't know how to react to someone who's upset, and more than half of teenagers don't know how to express their feelings – they can only stick to the facts when they talk about their problems.

According to the Samaritans' 1999 report *Young Men Speak Out*, the rates of male suicide in all age groups and in most countries have shown a striking increase since the 1970s, but this is most marked among 15- to 24-year-olds. In many parts of the world, in this age group it has become the second most frequent cause of death after accident.

As most secondary teachers know, things that seem insignificant or even trivial to adults can be of monumental importance to young people, who may get them totally out of proportion. It is important therefore to recognise and take seriously young people's worries even if they appear to be over the top to us as adults.

The ChildLine report suggests that the greatest risk of a repeat suicide attempt is within a few months of the first. Young people pretend they are fine and recovered, and their family are so relieved that their child survived that they develop a false sense of optimism. Young people are especially vulnerable in the period following action against people who have bullied them or hurt them in some other way. This is the time that schools can play an important role in making sure that their vigilance is heightened. Unfortunately, the calls that ChildLine receives suggest a very different story, with many callers feeling let down by people to whom they have gone for help and support.

How to broach the subject

If you have a concern that a young person is feeling suicidal, approach them; do not wait for them to come forward, as they may not feel able to. Tell them that you are concerned about them and ask what is wrong. ChildLine makes the following suggestions:

Ask: 'How do you feel?' or 'How bad do you feel?'

Say: 'Sometimes people feel suicidal; do you ever feel like that?'

If the young person displays anger at your suggestion that something may be wrong, don't take this to mean that you are wrong to have the concern. Young people in this situation may not be able to accept the first offer of help, especially if they have been let down by others they have sought help from.

If the young person storms off refusing to talk to you, don't give up on them, try again.

Say: 'I am sorry I upset you but I am still concerned about you.' If the young person still refuses to talk to you, try to help them identify someone whom they could talk to; you might suggest ChildLine if they feel that they cannot talk to someone face-to-face.

Some young people find it easier to write things down rather than telling someone directly, and some young people are better talking while they are doing some form of activity, rather than having to make eye contact.

If the young person starts telling you what is troubling them, listen and take it seriously, and make it clear that you care about them. Don't make light of it or be judgemental. Don't assume that intelligence will protect someone from suicidal thoughts.

TEACHING EXPERTISE

Confidentiality

If a young person talks to a member of staff about wanting to commit suicide, there can be no room for total confidentiality. Try to help the young person identify who needs to know about their concerns/worries/ depression, but make it clear that you cannot keep it confidential. Try to encourage the young person to talk to people who care for them; you might offer to be with them when they tell, but make sure they understand that if they are not able to say anything, you will have to, because you care about them. If a young person says they will talk to their parent or another carer you need to check that they have done so. Remember: The ground rule in child protection is that you cannot unknow what you have come to know.

Consider who you will need to talk to, this may include: the young person's parents, children's social care, CAMHS, the young person's GP, school nurse, school counsellor. Check your confidentiality policy for advice about young people expressing suicidal thoughts; does it cover this scenario?

Peer group support

Many schools have developed peer counselling support networks, recognising that children and young people may feel more able to talk to their peer group. Young people involved in offering such support need to know what to do if they think a young person may be contemplating suicide. Some schools run a listening service, for example, with active listening skills training for young people so that they can be available in small teams at set times to offer support to other young people in the school.

ChildLine reports that they get a large number of calls from young people concerned about their friend. Where this happens in school, such concerns should be taken seriously and reported to the named child protection person. Friends often need a lot of reassurance that they have done the right thing in telling and may need ongoing support and in some cases counselling.

ChildLine runs an outreach project called CHIPS (ChildLine in Partnership with Schools), which works with more than 800 secondary schools to help young people get involved in issues that affect their lives. These may include anti-bullying and anti-racism strategies. CHIPS encourages children and young people to be a source of help for each other by running – for instance – befriending and peer support.

The Internet

Some young people will seek help from the Internet. There are plenty of websites about suicide, many of which aim to help people through periods of suicidal thoughts, but young people do need guidance about which would be most appropriate:

Here are some useful sites that help young people to manage their mental health issues:

⇨ Childline: www.childline.org.uk, or tel: 0800 1111

⇨ Young Minds: www.youngminds.org.uk

⇨ Samaritans: www.samaritans.org, or tel: 08457 90 90 90

⇨ Get Connected: www.getconnected.org.uk, or tel: 0808 808 4994

⇨ Papyrus: www.papyrus-uk.org, or tel Hopeline UK: 0800 068 41 41.

Next steps

Schools can take an active role in suicide prevention by:

⇨ developing a listening and helping ethos.

⇨ ensuring that all staff know how to report their concerns or information about young people at risk of suicide.

⇨ developing peer group counselling.

⇨ developing strong links with helping agencies.

⇨ making sure helpline numbers such as ChildLine and Samaritans are displayed.

⇨ taking young people's concerns seriously.

June 2008

⇨ The above information is reprinted with kind permission from teachingexpertise. Visit www. teachingexpertise.com for more information.

© *teachingexpertise*

TEACHINGEXPERTISE

Childhood adversities are 'powerful predictors' of suicide

Information from the Royal College of Psychiatrists.

Children who experience physical or sexual abuse, or other adversities such as the death of a parent or family violence, are at greater risk of suicide in later life, according to new research. And the greater the number of different adversities a child experiences, the more they are at risk.

Researchers, writing in the July issue of the *British Journal of Psychiatry*, describe childhood adversities as a 'powerful predictor' of suicidal behaviour.

The team, led by Dr Ronny Bruffaerts from Katholieke Universiteit Leuven in Belgium, examined data from the World Mental Health surveys carried out in 21 countries in Africa, the Americas, Asia and the Pacific, Europe, and the Middle East.

Children who experience physical or sexual abuse, or other adversities such as the death of a parent or family violence, are at greater risk of suicide in later life, according to new research

More than 55,000 people from all 21 countries were interviewed about their experiences during childhood. They were asked if they had experienced any of the following adversities before the age of 18: physical abuse, sexual abuse, neglect, parental death, parent divorce, other parental loss, family violence, physical illness and financial adversity.

The researchers found that many of the people in the study had experienced adversity: 12% had experienced the death of a parent, 8% had been the victim of physical abuse and 7% of family violence.

Almost 3% of people interviewed said they had attempted suicide, and 9% said they had thought about killing themselves (known as suicide ideation). Among those who had tried to kill themselves, nearly a third (29%) had been the victim of physical abuse, one in four (25%) had experienced family violence, and one in six (15%) had been sexually abused.

Dr Bruffaerts said: 'We found that being exposed to many different adversities during childhood increases the risk of suicidal behaviour. Sexual or physical abuses during childhood are particularly strong risk factors for the onset of suicidal behaviour in adulthood. Even controlling for a broad set of variables, there was at least a threefold increase in suicide attempt and suicide ideation among people with a history of sexual or physical abuse.'

Dr Bruffaerts concluded: 'Across the world, great emphasis is placed on the prevention of suicide. Our study shows a direct association between the number of adversities a person experiences in childhood and the risk of suicide. Therefore, identifying those families at risk of problems, and offering help, may be a way of decreasing suicide around the world.'

July 2010

⇨ The above information is reprinted with kind permission from the Royal College of Psychiatrists. Visit www.rcpsych.ac.uk for more information.

© Royal College of Psychiatrists

ROYAL COLLEGE OF PSYCHIATRISTS

Suicide and the media

Information from Befrienders Worldwide.

Samaritans UK/ROI believes responsible discussion of suicide on the Internet and in the media can lead to a better understanding of suicidal behaviour and the value of expressing feelings. In the UK, 29% of people know someone who has taken their own life, and enabling someone to talk openly about suicidal thoughts is an important step in breaking down the taboo.

However, glamorising suicide or providing 'how to'-type advice about suicide on the Internet, as in other forms of media, is potentially very dangerous. Although there is little research as yet to prove that there is a link between people visiting suicide chat rooms and taking their own lives, research carried out into the portrayal of suicide in traditional media, such as television, magazines and newspapers shows that there is a direct link between the way in which suicide is discussed and vulnerable people's behaviour. A number of recent cases highlighted in the media seem to indicate that there is a link, but research needs to be carried out to establish the extent and exact nature of it.

Anyone in emotional distress, or actively thinking about suicide is vulnerable and often looking for help in any form. Samaritans strongly encourages anyone publishing material about suicide to follow these guidelines:

⇨ Do not show or explain the method of suicide.

⇨ Do not emphasise potential positive results of killing oneself.

⇨ Do not trivialise suicide or portray it as an easy way out.

The Internet is an important medium for discussion about suicide and for providing support. But it can be difficult to know what the motives of people who are visiting suicide chat rooms or web sites are and whether they are being honest in their contributions. Vulnerable people could be influenced by people who are in these cyber spaces for another reason than seeking help or supporting others.

The UK Suicide Act of 1961 states that is illegal to aid, abet, counsel or procure the suicide of another and Samaritans strongly encourages anyone publishing material on the Internet to do so in a responsible way.

Samaritans UK/ROI offers confidential, emotional support by email on jo@samaritans.org. Launched in 2002, the number of contacts received by Samaritans email service in 2003 was nearly 100,000, an increase of 38% from 2002. The Samaritans' and Befrienders' websites are a source of information and support for anyone who wants information about the issues of suicide and how to get help. Evidence suggests that there are many benefits to using the Internet as a way of providing support for people in distress.

⇨ The anonymity of communicating by email means that people generally feel less frightened of being judged or rejected than in face-to-face circumstances or through speaking on the phone.

⇨ Many people who cannot access help by phone because they are worried about being heard or the phone number appearing on the bill can get in touch using email.

> *In the UK, 29% of people know someone who has taken their own life, and enabling someone to talk openly about suicidal thoughts is an important step in breaking down the taboo*

⇨ Online support helps people in distress to imagine the person answering the email in the most beneficial way possible. For example, those who would prefer someone younger to be answering the email can imagine the volunteer in that way, whilst those who would prefer someone older can imagine someone like that

⇨ It is recognised that writing is, in itself, a useful tool. The process of writing something down enables people to focus fully on their own feelings without worrying about taking up another person's time or saying the wrong thing.

Samaritans UK/ROI currently has a relationship with the ISP Wanadoo, whereby when anyone types a term into its search engine relating to suicide (e.g. suicide, or I want to kill myself), Samaritans UK/ROI is given a prominent advertisement-style listing above their other search results. Samaritans UK/ROI has now replicated this relationship with AOL and we also very much hope that other ISPs and search engine organisations, such as Yahoo and MSN follow suit.

⇨ The above information is reprinted with kind permission from Befrienders Worldwide. Visit www.befrienders.org for more information.

© The Samaritans

BEFRIENDERS WORLDWIDE

Copycat suicides and media reporting

Information from The Samaritans.

Suicide is a valid subject for discussion but certain types of suicide reporting are particularly harmful and can act as a catalyst to influence the behaviour of people who are already vulnerable.

Over 60 research articles have looked at the issue of media reporting of suicide and found that it can lead to imitative behaviours.

⇨ An episode of a popular TV drama contained a storyline about a deliberate self-poisoning with paracetamol. Researchers interviewed patients who attended Accident and Emergency departments and psychiatric services and found that 20% said the programme had influenced their decision to take an overdose. Self-poisoning increased by 17% in the week following the broadcast and by 9% in the second week.

⇨ A newspaper report in Hong Kong included a detailed description of a person who died by suicide involving the method of burning charcoal in a confined space. Within three years there was a dramatic increase in suicides using this method, with the number of deaths rising from 0% to 10%.

⇨ There has been an increase in the number of intentional antifreeze poisonings reported to the British National Poisons Information Service on two separate occasions, both of which followed reports on this method in the national media. The expected rate of self-poisoning by this method is between one and three per month. After the report of an inquest into a suicide using this method appeared in the national media, this rose to six cases in copycat suicides and media reporting in one month, and on a separate occasion when the method was portrayed in a popular hospital drama, the rate for that month leapt to nine.

⇨ A German television series, *Death of a student*, depicted the railway suicide of a young man at the start of each episode. A 175% rise in railway suicides occurred in young people aged 15-19 years old both during and after the series. This effect was repeated when the series was shown again some years later.

Positive examples

⇨ Studies in Vienna and Toronto found that voluntary restrictions on newspaper reporting of subway suicides resulted in a 75% decrease in suicides by this method.

⇨ A study following the death of singer Kurt Cobain by suicide found that there was not an overall increase in suicides rates in his home town of Seattle, believed to be because reporting differentiated strongly between the brilliance of his life achievements and the wastefulness of his death. It may have also helped that media coverage discussed risk factors and identified sources of help for people experiencing suicidal feelings.

Summary

Research suggests that media portrayal can influence suicidal behaviour and this may result in an overall increase in suicide and/or an increase in uses of particular methods. 'Perhaps the most important guiding principle for all journalists reporting suicide is to consider the vulnerable reader who might be in crisis when they see the story. We need to ask ourselves whether our coverage will make it more likely that they will attempt to take their lives or more likely that they will seek help. These excellent guidelines can help us make the right decisions.' Stephen Pritchard, Readers' Editor at the *Observer*, said.

⇨ The above information is reprinted with kind permission from The Samaritans. Visit www.samaritans.org.uk for more information.

© The Samaritans

THE SAMARITANS

DPP releases assisted suicide guidelines

Distinction must be drawn between those who help a loved one to kill themselves and those who end a life, says Keir Starmer.

By Haroon Siddique and agencies

Rules on assisted suicide intended to clarify when helping someone to end their life will result in prosecution will be published today after almost 5,000 people responded to the interim policy.

The eight pages of guidelines will be released by Keir Starmer QC, the Director of Public Prosecutions (DPP), this morning along with a 45-page summary of responses, the vast majority of which were from individual members of the public, according to the Crown Prosecution Service.

Assisted suicide remains a criminal offence in England and Wales, punishable by up to 14 years in prison, but individual decisions on prosecution are made depending on the circumstances in each case. An interim policy was published in September and has been in force since.

> **[The guidelines] made clear that someone acting out of compassion, to help a terminally ill patient with a 'clear, settled and informed wish to die' was unlikely to face the courts**

It made clear that someone acting out of compassion, to help a terminally ill patient with a 'clear, settled and informed wish to die' was unlikely to face the courts. But persuading or pressuring the victim to kill themselves, or benefiting from their death, would encourage prosecution.

Starmer was forced to issue the guidelines after a Law Lords ruling in favour of Debbie Purdy, who has multiple sclerosis.

She wanted to know whether her husband would be prosecuted for helping her to end her life.

Writing in the *Times*, the DPP said the recent debate about 'mercy killing' made it important to draw the line between those who help a loved one to kill themselves and suspects who have ended someone else's life.

'Assisted suicide involves assisting the victim to take his or her own life,' he wrote. 'Someone who takes the life of another undertakes a very different act and may well be liable to a charge of murder or manslaughter. That distinction is an important one that we all need to understand.

'Each case is unique, each case has to be considered on its own facts and merits; and prosecutors have to make professional judgements about difficult and sensitive issues. The assisted suicide policy will help them in that task.'

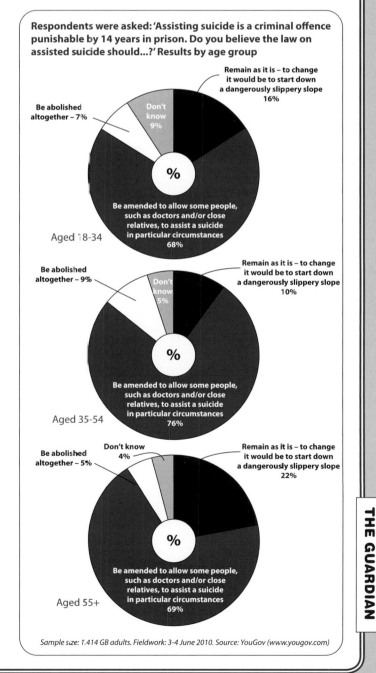

Respondents were asked: 'Assisting suicide is a criminal offence punishable by 14 years in prison. Do you believe the law on assisted suicide should...?' Results by age group

Aged 18-34
- Remain as it is – to change it would be to start down a dangerously slippery slope 16%
- Be amended to allow some people, such as doctors and/or close relatives, to assist a suicide in particular circumstances 68%
- Be abolished altogether – 7%
- Don't know 9%

Aged 35-54
- Remain as it is – to change it would be to start down a dangerously slippery slope 10%
- Be amended to allow some people, such as doctors and/or close relatives, to assist a suicide in particular circumstances 76%
- Be abolished altogether – 9%
- Don't know 5%

Aged 55+
- Remain as it is – to change it would be to start down a dangerously slippery slope 22%
- Be amended to allow some people, such as doctors and/or close relatives, to assist a suicide in particular circumstances 69%
- Be abolished altogether – 5%
- Don't know 4%

Sample size: 1,414 GB adults. Fieldwork: 3-4 June 2010. Source: YouGov (www.yougov.com)

THE GUARDIAN

He said that he found 'compelling' the large number of responses arguing 'that the factors tending against prosecution should focus more on the suspect than on the individual who committed suicide'.

Campaigners for the right to die welcomed the initial guidelines and called for the Government to legislate on the issue, but ministers were reluctant to intervene. Critics have complained Starmer is effectively legalising assisted suicide.

The Prime Minister, Gordon Brown, writing in a newspaper yesterday, said changing the law would 'fundamentally change' attitudes to death and could lead to pressure being put on frail elderly relatives. Purdy said his intervention showed a 'lack of respect' to the public.

Scope, a charity for disabled people, warned its members were 'genuinely frightened' about any changes that would weaken existing safeguards.

The chief executive, Richard Hawkes, said: 'We recognise that assisted suicide is a complex and emotional issue. However, as a charity which supports thousands of disabled people with complex support needs, we are very concerned about the potential impact of the DPP's new guidelines on assisted suicide.'

25 February 2010

© Guardian News and Media Ltd

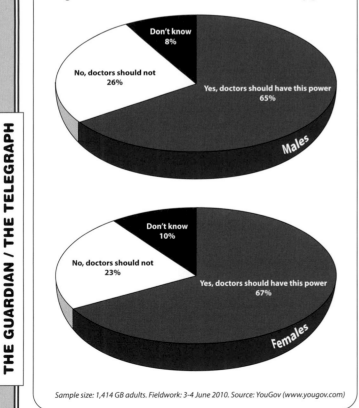

Respondents were asked: 'Do you think doctors should have the legal power to end the life of a terminally ill patient who has given a clear indication of a wish to die?'. Results by gender

Don't know
8%

No, doctors should not
26%

Yes, doctors should have this power
65%

Males

Don't know
10%

No, doctors should not
23%

Yes, doctors should have this power
67%

Females

Sample size: 1,414 GB adults. Fieldwork: 3-4 June 2010. Source: YouGov (www.yougov.com)

Assisted suicide: the law

Despite it being legal for a person to take their own life, under the 1961 Suicide Act, aiding or abetting someone to do so carries a potential jail term of up to 14 years.

By Richard Edwards

It is one of the more controversial laws and has been subject to hundreds of challenges and appeals.

The High Court has suggested that Parliament should review the law after the multiple sclerosis sufferer Debbie Purdy failed to force the Director of Public Prosecutions to give definitive guidance on whether those assisting loved ones to commit suicide would be prosecuted.

More than 100 British citizens have now taken advantage of Swiss laws that allow them to die with help from doctors and nurses at the Dignitas clinic in Zurich.

The Crown Prosecution Service decision not to press charges against the parents of Daniel James is unprecedented, but it was also justified by several caveats – including that they had helped him to fulfil his wish to die, against their own wishes.

More than 100 British citizens have now taken advantage of Swiss assisted suicide laws

The campaign group Dignity in Dying welcomed the decision not to prosecute and called for the law to be clarified.

Sarah Wootton, the organisation's chief executive, said: 'We fully agree that it is not in the public interest to bring a prosecution against Mr and Mrs James, but it is in the public interest to seek answers to the questions that this case and others like it raise.

'Due to a lack of a safeguarded choice, people are forced into making desperate and often dangerous decisions, people are travelling abroad to die, there are "mercy killings", botched suicides and some doctors already assist their patients to die at great potential cost to their livelihood and freedom.'

9 December 2008

© Telegraph Media Group Limited 2010

THE GUARDIAN / THE TELEGRAPH

Disabled people need help to live, not die

MPs must listen to the fears of disabled and terminally ill people and protect them from changes to the law on assisted suicide.

By Jane Campbell

I've been a campaigner for most of my life. I've not been alone. I've worked with other disabled people and great allies in parliament and elsewhere. Mostly, what we've wanted for disabled people has been almost universally applauded: better access, more support, equal rights. Opposition came from those holding the purse strings but we kept badgering away, arguing that equality for disabled people was good for everyone in society. By strength in numbers we scored notable victories, such as the Disability Discrimination Act. The wider public accepted that it was wrong for disabled people to receive inferior treatment.

Disabled people are still campaigning but this time we don't want change. We're united in wanting to keep things the same. How does one argue for the status quo? Chanting, 'What to de want?' 'No change', 'When do we want it?', 'Always' seems absurd.

Why bother at all? Because this could be the most important campaign of all, truly a matter of life and death.

Disabled and terminally ill people have had to deal with fear, prejudice and discrimination since the beginning of time. Our lives have been devalued by statements such as 'he/she'd be better off dead'. In recent years, calls for a change to the law prohibiting assisted suicide have grown louder and more frequent. They capitalise on fear. Fear of pain, fear of loss of dignity, fear of being a burden. And, yes, fear of witnessing those fears being felt by those we know and love. The solution offered to the fear of disability and illness is final: suicide.

Yet suicide is not well thought of in our society. It is 'committed' by the mentally ill and those unable to face the future. In both cases, society does all that it can to prevent suicidal thoughts being enacted. Life is too precious to be solely entrusted to individual action. That society is willing to protect us, even from ourselves in times of personal crisis, defines our – and its – humanity.

However, those seeking a change to the law on assisted suicide say such ideals have no place when considering severely disabled and terminally ill people. Such lives, it seems, are not so precious: ending them prematurely should be a matter of individual choice. Perversely, if you can take your own life without assistance, society generally strives to protect you; but, if assistance to die is needed, they argue, it should be provided. The option to choose the time of one's death is to be reserved for those for whom assistance is required.

No equality there. Yet many see this as irrefutably logical and compassionate.

It was the realisation that the majority of disabled and terminally ill people were not being heard in this debate that led to the formation of Not Dead Yet UK. We joined with other groups in opposing the two most recent attempts to change the law. In each case the House of Lords was decisive in rejecting calls for assisted suicide. However, the euthanasia campaigners have vowed to try again in the current parliament.

If they can make it legal for the life of a single person to be prematurely ended, they will then seek to broaden the criteria. Once early death becomes an 'option', it will gain a respectability that will erode the resolve of many people experiencing personal difficulties. Not only will it enter our heads, it will also enter the heads of our families and friends, those who provide us with health and social care support and, ultimately, those holding the purse strings.

> **Suicide is not well thought of in our society. It is 'committed' by the mentally ill and those unable to face the future. In both cases, society does all that it can to prevent suicidal thoughts being enacted**

How much more convenient for all if turkeys see voting for Christmas as exercising personal choice. No wonder disabled and terminally ill people are fearful of all attempts to weaken the current law. For any change would fundamentally alter not only how we are seen but also how we are treated and the care that we receive.

Campaigning to keep things as they are, to keep us safe, is not easy to do or explain. But we have our chant, 'Nothing about us, without us'. Our lives must not be given away without our resistance being heard. Indeed, 'Resistance' is the name of the campaign we are launching today. We have a short, five-point charter we want all MPs to sign. It calls on them to listen to disabled and terminally ill people in their constituencies who fear any change to the current law. We know what it is to be close to death. We want help to live, not help to die.

3 June 2010

© Guardian News and Media Limited 2010

THE GUARDIAN

KEY FACTS

⇨ About one in ten young people will self-harm at some point, but it can occur at any age. It is more common in young women than men. Gay and bisexual people seem to be more likely to self-harm. (page 1)

⇨ Self-harm is more common in some sub-cultures – 'goths' seem to be particularly vulnerable. People who self-harm are more likely to have experienced physical, emotional or sexual abuse during childhood. (page 2)

⇨ 43% of respondents in one survey on self-harm reported self-hate being a motive. 45% reported harming in order to punish themselves. One in four participants reported feeling guilty, ashamed or embarrassed after an episode of self-harm. (page 10)

⇨ When asked how self-harm had helped them, 39% of participants in a survey wrote that it helped them regulate or release emotion. (page 11)

⇨ Most self-harm is hidden from others and motivated by private therapeutic needs rather than performed to achieve social or manipulative ends. (page 12)

⇨ Although women make up only 5% of the total prison population, they account for almost half the self-harm incidents in prison. (page 13)

⇨ Each year, around 25,000 admissions to hospitals in England and Wales are made by young people who have self-harmed. (page 14)

⇨ Self-harm is much more common than suicide. There are at least 140,000 attempted suicides each year in England and Wales. (page 20)

⇨ Men account for three-quarters of all suicides in the UK. Generally, men are more reluctant than women to talk about their feelings and to see their GP with psychological problems. (page 21)

⇨ Research has shown that almost all people who end their lives by suicide have a mental illness, most commonly depression. (page 21)

⇨ Attempted suicide is much higher amongst the unemployed than amongst people who are in work. This is also true of homeless people. Young gay men and lesbians are particularly at risk too, possibly because of the discrimination they face in our society. (page 24)

⇨ Doctors, nurses, pharmacists, vets and farmers have a higher risk of suicide than other professions. It's likely that this is connected to high stress, combined with easy access to the means of dying by suicide. (page 25)

⇨ Scotland's suicide rate is higher than rates in other parts of the UK. (page 26)

⇨ Serious talk about suicide does not create or increase risk, it reduces it. The best way to identify the possibility of suicide is to ask directly. (page 27)

⇨ A conservative estimate is that there are 24,000 cases of attempted suicide by adolescents (10-19 years) each year in England and Wales, which is one attempt every 20 minutes. (page 31)

⇨ Children who experience physical or sexual abuse, or other adversities such as the death of a parent or family violence, are at greater risk of suicide in later life. (page 34)

⇨ 29% of people in the UK know someone who has taken their own life. (page 35)

⇨ Research suggests that media portrayal can influence suicidal behaviour and this may result in an overall increase in suicide and/or an increase in uses of particular methods. (page 36)

⇨ Assisted suicide remains a criminal offence in England and Wales, punishable by up to 14 years in prison, but individual decisions on prosecution are made depending on the circumstances in each case. (page 37)

Assisted suicide

Assisted suicide refers to an individual who has a terminal, chronic or life-limiting condition enlisting a relative, friend or medical professional to help them take their own life. The person who assists them can be charged with a criminal act, as although it is legal to commit suicide, under the 1961 Suicide Act, aiding or abetting someone to do so carries a potential jail term of up to 14 years. Cases of prosecution for assisted suicide are often hotly debated, and euthanasia (sometimes referred to as 'mercy killing') remains a highly controversial subject.

Bipolar disorder

Previously called manic depression, this illness is characterised by mood swings where periods of severe depression are balanced by periods of elation and overactivity (mania).

Cognitive behavioural therapy (CBT)

A psychological treatment which assumes that behavioural and emotional reactions are learned over a long period. A cognitive therapist will seek to identify the source of emotional problems and develop techniques to overcome them.

Copycat suicides

In rare cases, an individual may choose to take their own life because they have heard about others doing so, or have been exposed to suicide via the media. Or they may choose to commit suicide using a particular method they have become aware of due to media exposure. A famous recent example is the spate of copycat suicides which took place in Bridgend, Wales, in 2008, when a total of approximately 24 teenagers took their lives, the majority of whom did not know each other. Internet suicide 'cults' or 'pacts' have also been blamed for serial suicides.

Depression

Someone is said to be significantly depressed, or suffering from depression, when feelings of sadness or misery don't go away quickly and are so bad that they interfere with everyday life. Symptoms can also include low self-esteem and a lack of motivation.

Group therapy

These are meetings for people who are seeking help for a problem (in this case, self-harm or suicidal thoughts) and are led by trained specialists. They differ from self-help groups in that an expert is present to run the meeting and provide professional advice and support.

Overdosing

Overdosing involves taking a larger quantity of a particular drug or medication than is safe, sometimes inadvertently but often as an act of self-harm (this may be referred to as self-poisoning) or as an attempt to kill oneself. Although overdoses don't always lead to death, sometimes the drugs ingested can cause irreversible damage to the liver and other vital organs.

Self-harm/self-injury

Self-harm is the act of deliberately injuring or mutilating oneself. People injure themselves in many different ways, including cutting, burning, poisoning or hitting parts of their body. Self-harmers often see harming as a coping strategy and give a variety of motivations for hurting themselves, including relieving stress or anxiety, focusing emotional pain and as a way of feeling in control. Although prevalent in young people, self-harm is found amongst patients of all ages. It is not usually an attempt to commit suicide, although people who self-harm are statistically more likely to take their own lives than those who don't.

Suicide

Suicide is the act of taking one's own life. Men are statistically more likely to take their own life than women, and suffering from a mental illness such as depression, bipolar disorder or schizophrenia is also a risk factor for suicide. Elderly people are also considered vulnerable as they are more likely to have to deal with traumatic life events such as bereavement and ill health.

Talking therapies

These involve talking and listening. Some therapists will aim to find the root cause of a sufferer's problem and help them deal with it, some will help to change behaviour and negative thoughts, while others simply offer support.

Additional Resources

Other Issues titles

If you are interested in researching further some of the issues raised in *Self-Harming and Suicide,* you may like to read the following titles in the *Issues* series:

➪ Vol. 192 *Bereavement and Grief* (ISBN 978 1 86168 543 8)

➪ Vol. 190 *Coping with Depression* (ISBN 978 1 86168 541 4)

➪ Vol. 184 *Understanding Eating Disorders* (ISBN 978 1 86168 525 4)

➪ Vol. 179 *Tackling Child Abuse* (ISBN 978 1 86168 503 2)

➪ Vol. 176 *Health Issues for Young People* (ISBN 978 1 86168 500 1)

➪ Vol. 170 *Body Image and Self-Esteem* (ISBN 978 1 86168 484 4)

➪ Vol. 165 *Bullying Issues* (ISBN 978 1 86168 469 1)

➪ Vol. 152 *Euthanasia and the Right to Die* (ISBN 978 1 86168 439 4)

➪ Vol. 141 *Mental Health* (ISBN 978 1 86168 407 3)

➪ Vol. 100 *Stress and Anxiety* (ISBN 978 1 86168 314 4)

For a complete list of available *Issues* titles, please visit our website: www.independence.co.uk/shop

Useful organisations

You may find the websites of the following organisations useful for further research:

➪ **Befrienders Worldwide:** www.befrienders.org

➪ **Console:** www.console.ie

➪ **Lesbian and Gay Foundation:** www.lgf.org.uk

➪ **Mental Health Foundation:** www.mentalhealth.org.uk

➪ **Mind:** www.mind.org.uk

➪ **NHS Choices:** www.nhs.uk

➪ **Royal College of Psychiatrists:** www.rcpsych.ac.uk

➪ **SANE:** www.sane.org.uk

➪ **Scottish Public Health Observatory:** www.scotpho.org.uk

➪ **See Me Scotland:** www.seemescotland.org.uk

➪ **teachingexpertise:** www.teachingexpertise.com

➪ **TES:** www.tes.co.uk

➪ **The Samaritans:** www.samaritans.org.uk

➪ **TheSite:** www.thesite.org

➪ **YouthNet:** www.youthnet.org

For more book information, visit our website...

www.independence.co.uk

Information available online includes:

✓ Detailed descriptions of titles

✓ Tables of contents

✓ Facts and figures

✓ Online ordering facilities

✓ Log-in page for Issues Online (an Internet resource available free to Firm Order Issues subscribers – ask your librarian to find out if this service is available to you)

ACKNOWLEDGEMENTS

The publisher is grateful for permission to reproduce the following material.

While every care has been taken to trace and acknowledge copyright, the publisher tenders its apology for any accidental infringement or where copyright has proved untraceable. The publisher would be pleased to come to a suitable arrangement in any such case with the rightful owner.

Chapter One: Self-Harm

Self-harm, © Royal College of Psychiatrists, Self-injury: myths and common sense, © National Self-Harm Network, The truth about self-harm, © Mental health Foundation, Coping tips and distractions, © TheSite. org, Before and after an episode of self-harm [graphs], © SANE, Selina's story: 'I wanted to punish myself for being such a failure', © The Independent, Understanding self-harm, © SANE, Function of self-harm [graph], © SANE, What happens at A&E?, © TheSite.org, Self-harm in women's prisons, © Crown copyright is reproduced with the permission of Her Majesty's Stationery Office, New report highlights self-harm needs to be taken more seriously, © The Lesbian and Gay Foundation, Motivations and their prevalence in driving acts of self-harm, Time since first episode of self-harm [graphs], © SANE, Self-harm makes its mark on pre-teens, © TES, NHS services 'failing to support people who self-harm', © Royal College of Psychiatrists, Websites told to remove material promoting self-harm, © Guardian News and Media Limited 2010.

Chapter Two: Suicide

Suicide, © Crown Copyright is reproduced with the permission of Her Majesty's Stationery Office – nhs.uk, How to help someone who is suicidal, © Mind, Suicide in Scotland: key points, © Scottish Public Health Observatory, Suicide myths, © See Me Scotland, Suicide: young men at risk, © Crown Copyright is reproduced with the permission of Her Majesty's Stationery Office – nhs.uk, Warning signs of suicidal behaviour, © Console, Number of suicide and undetermined deaths in UK and ROI 1999-2008 [graph], © The Samaritans, Understanding and preventing suicide in young people, © teachingexpertise, Childhood adversities are 'powerful predictors' of suicide, © Royal College of Psychiatrists, Suicide and the media, © The Samaritans, Copycat suicides and media reporting, © Samaritans, DPP releases assisted suicide guidelines, © Guardian News and Media Limited 2010, Assisted suicide survey [graphs], © YouGov, Assisted suicide: the law, © Telegraph Media Group Limited 2010, Disabled people need help to live, not die, © Guardian News and Media Limited 2010.

Illustrations

Pages 1, 11, 17, 33: Angelo Madrid; pages 5, 19: Bev Aisbett; pages 8, 15, 29, 36: Don Hatcher; pages 9, 14, 23, 34: Simon Kneebone.

Cover photography

Left: © Andrzej Gdula. Centre: © Hazel Brown. Right: © T. Al Nakib.

Additional acknowledgements

Research and additional editorial by Carolyn Kirby on behalf of Independence.

And with thanks to the Independence team: Mary Chapman, Sandra Dennis and Jan Sunderland.

Lisa Firth
Cambridge
September, 2010